OUTER CIRCLE

BIRMINGHAM'S
No.11 BUS ROUTE

OUTER CIRCLE

BIRMINGHAM'S
No.11 BUS ROUTE

DAVID HARVEY, MARGARET HANSON
& PETER DRAKE

TEMPUS

Frontispiece: When the Outer Circle No.11 bus route was first completed on 7 April 1926, a good deal of the northern and eastern parts of the route ran through what was still open countryside. Loading up with passengers in Stechford Lane is bus 176 (OP 205). This AEC 504 had a Short Brothers outside staircase, a fifty-two seat body and a 6.8 litre petrol engine, which managed about 4 m.p.h. It entered service on 1 September of the same year as the Circle was completed. Behind the bus, which is still on rubber tyres, is the recently reconstructed Fox and Goose public house. 176 was withdrawn at the end of January 1935, though it had run for over half its life on pneumatic tyres. (J. Whybrow)

First published 2003

Tempus Publishing Limited
The Mill, Brimscombe Port,
Stroud, Gloucestershire, GL5 2QG

British Library Cataloguing in Publication Data.
A catalogue record for this book is available from the British Library.

ISBN 0 7524 3081 5

Typesetting and origination by Tempus Publishing Limited
Printed in Great Britain by Midway Colour Print, Wiltshire

Contents

Introduction   6

one   The Circle Starts: 9
Lordswood Road to Cotteridge

two   Stirchley to Swanshurst   37

three   Sarehole to Yardley   55

four   South Yardley to Six Ways Erdington   77

five   Reservoir Road to Church Lane   105

six   Completing the Circle: 129
Oxhill Road to the Kings Head

seven   The Outer Circle Garages   153

Acknowledgements   160

Picture Credits   160

Introduction

What measures twenty-six miles, goes round in circles and ends up where it started? Alternatively, what goes round in circles and takes twenty million passengers for a ride each year? Journalists asked to produce copy for an article about the Outer Circle route have usually fallen back on these or similar questions to preface their writing. So why buck the tradition? After all, the No.11 has been going round now for nearly eighty years, so traditions are appropriate. Readers of this book will love the statistics about the Outer Circle, so let's start with, appropriately, eleven facts and statistics about the route:

- Over 50,000 customers travel on the route every day.
- It is twenty-six miles long and, on average, four miles distant from the city centre. Only the short stretch in Bearwood is outside the city's boundary.
- Forty-two buses operate on the route, covering a combined 44,000 miles every week.
- It takes two hours and twenty minutes to travel the circle.
- There are 266 stops along the route.
- Forty pubs, nineteen suburban shopping centres and six hospitals are on the route, which crosses all the main arterial roads radiating from the city centre.
- The No.11 route is one of Europe's longest bus routes. Winson Green is the nearest point to the city centre and Cotteridge the furthest.
- A total of 111 drivers are employed to operate the service.
- An Outer Circle walk, sponsored by Lewis's, was held annually in July from 1928 to 1974.
- Three of the great British literary figures of the twentieth century – the poet W.H. Auden, the literary and theatre critic Kenneth Tynan and J.R.R. Tolkien – all had their childhood homes on or very close to the route, while the greatest reader of a comedy sketch, Tony Hancock, was born close to the Hall Green stretch.
- Simon Le Bon from the group Duran Duran composed the hit single 'Hungry Like the Wolf' on the No.11 bus travelling from Perry Barr to Kings Heath. Martin Barre, guitarist with Jethro Tull, composed the instrumental 'The Outer Circle' (on his album 'The Meeting') inspired by memories of his days travelling to gigs on the No.11.

The circle came into operation on Wednesday 7 April 1926. It had its origins in two routes introduced in January 1923: the No.10 route from Kings Heath via Cotteridge to the Kings Head and the No.11 route from Six Ways Erdington to Acocks Green and Moseley. When the No.11 service began running from Moseley Village to the Kings Head in February 1925, it was called the Outer Circle for the first time. The section between Acocks Green and Moseley was incorporated into the No.1A route and the No.10 route became the missing link of the Outer Circle when the route was completed.

So what has changed since 1926 and what has remained the same? The route itself, with a few minor changes, is virtually the same. Much of the scenery and the buildings along the route now would be instantly recognisable to a Twenties passenger, though sections of the route ran virtually through the countryside in places such as Bromford Lane, Hall Green and Harborne. The pubs, for example, are still largely the landmarks and the destination points they were when conductors would call out the various places of interest: 'The Swan' … 'The Yew Tree' … 'The Bull's Head' … 'The Bromford' … 'The Navigation' … and so on, all round the route. Unlike the street corner pubs on the Inner Circle route, the public houses on the No.11 route were large road houses. However several of them, such as the Yew Tree and the Manor Tavern, have been closed very recently or are being redeveloped. The No.11 is still convenient for the city's premier soccer venue, Villa Park; the speedway and greyhound racing at Hall Green and Perry Barr; HM Prison Winson Green; the Witton and Yardley cemeteries; and the major tourist attractions of Cadbury World, Sarehole Mill and Blakesley Hall. All the cinemas along the way, though, have been converted to different uses, such as bingo halls and gurdwaras. Schools on and just off the route provide a valuable source of passenger revenue in the daytime. However, aspects of the city's diverse culture would not have been apparent in the Twenties. The route can now boast an Iyengar yoga centre in Westley Road, a cross-dressing shop called Transformation in Oxhill Road and a Kurdistan hall in Rookery Road.

The northern and eastern parts of the route still have most of the industry and the south and the west the most expensive houses. Undoubtedly, the route is more built up since the Twenties. In fact, in the very early days of operation, many of the southern parts of the route were still rural and it was partly the development of the No.11 bus route that contributed to the growing suburbanisation of the city's outer ring. The construction of numerous stretches of dual carriageways catered for the new route and the subsequent increase in traffic. Like the trams before had done, the No.11 route was the catalyst which triggered the development new suburbs. Before the war, a trip on the Outer Circle was a genuine half-day out for residents and visitors to the city alike. Aware that Brummies could make a day trip to the Lickies on the No.70 tram, the No.11 bus route advertised itself thus: 'See Birmingham by bus – a new way to spend a half-holiday'. Conductors recall getting on at Kings Heath and finding the whole top deck full of 'all-rounders', the name for those travelling the whole route. There was even a special excursion rate available before 2.30 p.m. Leisure time seems these days to be spent on more sophisticated activities, but still anyone wanting to understand the geography of the city could have no better introduction than a ride around the circle on a No.11.

The two hours and ten minutes of the Outer Circle can be summed up in a few sentences. You start off from the Kings Head on Hagley Road, then it's on to Harborne, with the Queen Elizabeth Hospital complex on the left, past Cadbury's and Bournville and on to Kings Heath and Hall Green – which some would say is the prettiest stretch. Then it's on to Acocks Green, past Yardley cemetery to the Swan. Next you drop down to Stechford and the baths, followed by the industrial complexes at Bromford, and then under the M6 motorway and up to Erdington. You then visit Stockland Green, Witton cemetery, IMI and the Villa ground before Perry Barr. Next come more leafy roads in Handsworth Wood before crossing the Soho Road and then on to HMP Winson Green. Finally, you go across the Dudley Road into City Road and on to Bearwood, before going back to the Kings Head.

Bus crews have always regarded the route as something special. However, some have never got to grips with the steady ride round, and on Sundays it can be pretty monotonous. Back in the 1960s, one conductor found an unexpected reason for liking the route, saying: 'With thirty-nine different stages, each going to any of the others, there are 1,852 possible journeys, so we have to be pretty good at maths – but it does make the time pass quickly. Actually, I prefer the anti-clockwise direction – the inner ring we call it. Its fares are easier to calculate as the stages go up from one to thirty-nine instead of backwards.' Another driver recalls thinking he had spotted a cousin of his from Ireland working on the roads near the Swan and then having to drive another twenty-five miles and wait over two hours for confirmation – it was! Another anecdote involves spotting a good-looking table in a shop on one journey and making an unauthorised stop on the next to put down a deposit. Then there were the smoking breaks and the waiting points. And, of course, the perennial passenger complaint about the No.11 – having to wait for ages and then the buses turn up in convoy.

The buses themselves, of course, have developed over the eighty years. Although the original No.11 route was operated by tiny twenty-six seat Daimler CK2 single-deckers, state-of-the-art AEC 504 double-deckers were introduced after 7 April 1926. Can you imagine going around the No.11 route sitting on a garden seat inside a bus running on what are now called 'solid tyres'? The driver sits alongside the frequently smelly petrol engine wearing a greatcoat, gaiters and polished, knee-high leather boots; if it rains, he pulls a series of tarpaulins over and around him, in order to afford some protection from the elements, as there is no windscreen. On a cigarette smoke-filled top-deck, which is reached by what is little better than a semi-circular ladder, you get a distinctly firm ride thanks to the cart-spring suspension, as you rub a somewhat intimate shoulder with one of the other twenty-six passengers on the top-deck, who are sharing with you the joys of Corporation bus riding! Perhaps you might be aware that you are riding on a bus which looks very similar to the double-deckers running in the London of the Roaring Twenties but, unlike the passengers in the capital, you can offer up a silent prayer to Mr Baker, the General Manager, who had your bus equipped from new with a roof to the top deck, which protects you from the cold, the rain and occasionally the snow.

Move on thirty years to the Corporation buses of the1950s, which are, as always, immaculately coach painted and well maintained. The style of the post-war bus bodies had evolved from the pre-war ones that had been built locally by Metro-Cammell at Washwood Heath, or Birmingham Railway, Carriage and Wagon at Smethwick. They had a lower saloon equipped with moquette and leather-covered seats, which gave the apearance of a comfortable sitting room, while the leather and polished wood of the top deck, reached by way of a straight and easy-to-negotiate staircase from a wide, but still open rear platform, was akin to a gentlemen's smoking room. The driver was quite well catered for with probably the best and most subtly ventilated cab that was ever designed. Although he did not have the later luxury of power-steering, with a well-greased steering box and either a pleasant-to-drive synchromesh gearbox (on the post-war Crossleys and Leylands) or a pre-selector gearbox (fitted to the Daimlers and Guys), the Birmingham bus driver's life was better than most.

Throughout the life of Birmingham City Transport, the buses working on the No.11 route were crew operated, with both a driver and a conductor. That is why it was not until 31 October 1977, after the demise of the back-loaders (some of which were in their twenty-seventh year), that rear-engined, front-entrance Daimler Fleetlines – operated as one-person buses – became the regular buses performing on the by-now West Midlands P.T.E. In the last twenty years, the Outer Circle has been operated by M.C.W. Metrobuses, with some of the Mark I type lasting until 2003, when they were well over twenty years old. With the imminent showcasing of the Outer Circle, the latest Travel West Midlands Volvo B7Ls and Dennis Trident double-deckers will have either Alexander or Wright bodies. They have low floors, lowering platforms, air conditioning and air suspension. However, while they are splendid vehicles, they might not be as much fun as the buses of the 1920s and 1950s – or is nostalgia getting too much for us!

By the time this book is in print, work to upgrade the route will have started. It will be converted to Bus Showcase standards, with £25 million spent on brand-new low-floor buses, new shelters, real-time passenger information, bus lanes, bus priority at traffic lights and further safety features. The entire project should be completed by 2006. It all bears out the value of the Outer Circle route in moving people round the city, and should attract up to 2,000 trips a day, which would previously have been made by car. As an official of The West Midlands Passenger Travel Executive said of the No.11, when the route celebrated its half-century in 1976: 'It's like an important vein carrying blood around the body. We can't do without it'.

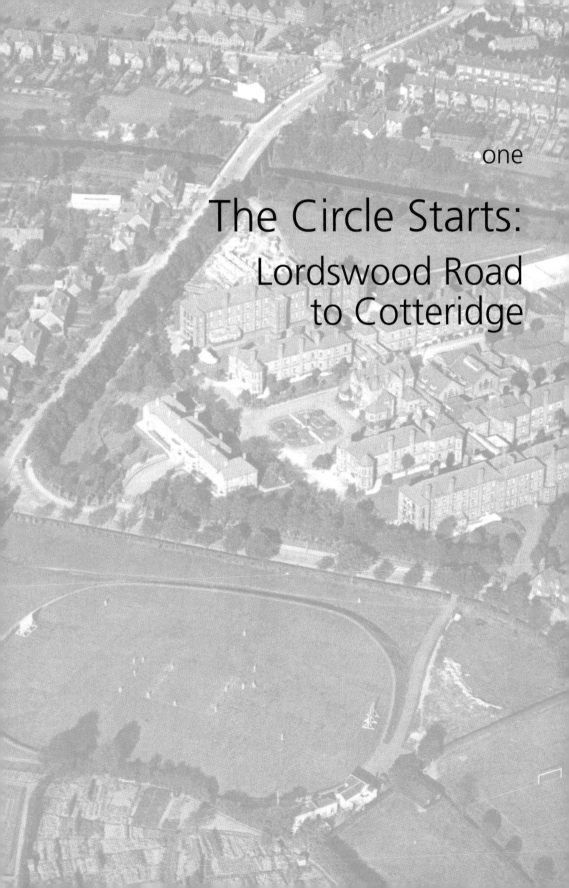

one

The Circle Starts:
Lordswood Road to Cotteridge

Above: The criticism in letters to the local press in the early 1930s that the Outer Circle was only worked by old buses had all but disappeared by the middle of that decade. One of the very early (the fourth, in fact) AEC Regent 661s with a totally-enclosed Brush 50 seat body is seen in Lordswood Road on 19 September 1935. It has just passed Kelmscott Road on the right with the bollards marking the entrance to Knightlow Road, halfway up the hill. These buses, of which there were thirty, were all delivered around the turn of 1930, with this vehicle entering service on 8 November 1929. It possessed a very early Regent chassis – numerically, the fifteenth to come out of the Southall works of AEC The chassis designer was G.J. Rackham, who had been headhunted from Leyland Motors, where he had designed the revolutionary Titan range of double-deckers in 1928. The 341 retained its petrol engine for the whole of its long life, being one of fifty Regents to be rebodied with Ministry of War Transport utility bodies, again built by Brush. It survived in this guise until 1950, operating from Birchfield Road garage, which was the only one to have facilities to refuel buses with petrol by that time. (Birmingham Central Library)

Opposite below: Having sped down Lordswood Road from the Kings Head, the first main stop was at the junction with Croftdown Road, where the No.10 route to Quinton Road West crossed the Outer Circle. In about 1965, a new-look front Crossley 2487 (JOJ 487), one of the last hundred DD42/7 chassis to be delivered to the Corporation (in this case entering service in August 1950), pulls up outside the Old House at the Home public house, just short of Gillhurst Road. The eighteenth-century pub, noted for its Rushton's Ales, was replaced by a much larger building in the inter-war period which corresponded with the widening of Lordswood Road into a wide-verged, tree-lined road, linking Bearwood to Harborne. 2487 was destined to be one of the last Crossleys in service with the Corporation, not being withdrawn until July 1969. (R.F. Mack)

Above: Opposite Croftdown Road and situated between Carless Avenue and Gillhurst Lane is the delightful local shop at 169 Lordswood Road, pictured in 1951. The footpath just to the left of the bus stop leads to Ravenhurst Road. The shop was owned by Miss Ellen Durkin in 1951, and Kelly's Directory shows that she had been there since 1923, when she was listed as jointly running the shop with Miss Beatrice Annett. The prominent sign in the front garden reads 'Hadley Brothers – Your Television Dealer'. However, the shop – with its signs advertising Colman's Mustard, Colman's Starch and Craven A Tobacco – seems to have traded as a general store. (Birmingham Central Library)

Above: A Guy Arab IV 2991 (JOJ 991) travels along Lordswood Road near the junction with Croftdown Road on 7 July 1966. It is travelling towards the Kings Head, where the crew will take a well-earned rest at the Bundy Clock. These buses had the 8.4 litre Gardner 6LW engine, which was coupled to a Wilson pre-selector gearbox and a fluid flywheel. The gearchange stick was mounted where a normal gear lever would have been found, though it could always be identified by being thinner and with a smaller knob than a conventional gear lever. These Guys were regular performers on the Outer Circle service for nearly twenty-five years and, with their solidly-built Metro-Cammell fifty-five seater bodies, always seemed to be masters of their task. 2991 spent nearly all of its B.C.T. life working from Acocks Green garage, and by 1966 had been modified by the cutting back of its front wings, as these buses – if they had an Achilles Heel – were prone to brake fade in hot weather. The shortened wings allowed more air onto the brakes, though it did little to improve their aesthetic front profile. (R.F. Mack)

Opposite above: Approaching Harborne Village in Lordswood Road at Lonsdale Road is a Leyland Titan PD2/1 1729 (HOV 729), which spent the whole of its twenty-year life operating from Perry Barr garage. Although these Leylands had synchromesh gearboxes and the Birmingham fleet was basically an easy-change fleet, with most buses being specified with fluid flywheels and Wilson pre-selector gearboxes, they were popular buses as they had very powerful Leyland 0.600 engines, which had a 9.8 litre capacity. 1729 was one of exactly one hundred such buses delivered with metal-framed Brush bodies in 1947 and 1948, specifically designed to Birmingham's rigorous specifications. However, no more bodies were ever ordered from Brush as they made a number of errors during the construction of the bodies, which did not endear them to the B.C.T. management. These mistakes included cutting the lower saloon moquette in such a way that the leaves and berries on the design grew sideways and not downwards! To the right, about seventy yards along Lonsdale Road, was the back entrance to Harborne garage, which was one of the three regular suppliers of all-day buses on the Outer Circle route. (R.F. Mack)

Above: Harborne Baths opened on 13 December 1928 with T.B. Wall as the officer in charge. The sign above the doors and below the Birmingham coat of arms advertises 'swimming bath, mixed bathing, and washing baths'. To the right of these doors, there is now a plaque to the poet W.H. Auden. Auden's father was the Chief Medical Officer for Health for the city, and the family home (now demolished) was next door to the baths. The plaque, which was erected by the Birmingham Civic Society, commemorates Auden's time in Harborne from 1919 to 1939. (Birmingham Central Library)

Above: A distant Metro-Cammell-bodied Daimler COG5 of 1935 vintage approaches the Duke of York public house when working on the anti-clockwise No.11 route. The pub, dating from the nineteenth century, was subsequently demolished and replaced by purpose-built luxury town houses. The pub had originally been owned by Atkinsons before being taken over by Mitchells & Butlers. (A. Spettigue)

Above: If a bus had heavy steering, life on the Outer Circle was not much fun for the driver, especially if the bus had a 'three-bell load', i.e. was full with standing passengers. Turning hard left out of Harborne Park Road and then having to turn around the island in the centre of Harborne and into Lordswood Road at the top of War Lane was hard work, but a skilled driver, using the 'push-pull' technique on the steering wheel, would make the job look easy. Leyland buses always seemed to have light steering, so a Brush-bodied PD2/1, with its powerful 9.8 litre engine would always be a bonus, save for the fact that it had a manual synchromesh gearbox. 1719 (HOV 719) negotiates the island on a clockwise, or outer journey on the No.11 route in 1965. (R.F. Mack)

Opposite above: One of Harborne garage's own new-look front Crossleys, 2509 (JOJ 509), stops at the toilets at the Duke of York stop in Lordswood Road, Harborne. Here, there will either be a comfort break or a change of crew. If it were the latter, the driver would inevitably alter the position of his seat and get himself comfortable whilst waiting for the conductor to fill in his way-bill and give two rings on the bell to tell him to start off on the way to Selly Oak by way of Harborne Park Road. With the exceptions of being fitted with flashing indicators and having had its wheel trims removed, in 1959 the Crossley is in basically its original condition with full-length front wings, gold fleet numbers and chrome radiator trim. It is being overtaken by a Hillman Minx Series IIIA. (D.R. Harvey)

Above: 2615 (JOJ 615), one of Acocks Green garage's Guy Arab III Specials, whose chassis was specially designed and built for B.C.T., is operating on a short-working back to Acocks Green in about 1967, with the inevitable 'service extra' destination display. With their straight-through exhaust pipes booming through the single-lane section of Harborne Park Road immediately after leaving the Duke of York in Harborne, the noise these buses made in a confined space, such as this one, had to be heard to be believed, sounding as though someone had turned on the afterburners of an Avro Vulcan bomber! Well, that may be a slight exaggeration, but they 'didn't half rasp!' (R.F. Mack)

Above: An AEC 504 with a Short H26/26RO body, 154 (OM 9568) travels up Harborne Park Road at the end of the dual carriageway section near Vivian Road. The bus is alongside Harborne Cricket and Hockey Club; this club was formed in 1868 and moved to its present site alongside Old Church Avenue in 1874. When the Outer Circle was first completed on 7 April 1926, it was these AEC double-deckers which took over from the tiny twenty-four seat Daimler CK2 single-deckers and transformed the service. Initially running on what today would be termed solid tyres, though in fact they should be called rubber tyres, these buses were a revelation. It has to be remembered that outside London, double-deckers were something of a rarity in the early 1920s, while ones with enclosed upper saloons, enabling the passengers on the top deck to get a dry ride, were to be found in experimental ones and twos elsewhere. In Birmingham, there were a fleet of around 200 of them available for service by the time the No.11 route began running. Ironically, with the introduction of the totally enclosed AEC Regent 661s in 1929, they were made obsolete virtually overnight, resulting in letters to the local press about the uncomfortable ride these four-year-old buses were giving. (Birmingham Central Library)

Opposite below: Harborne Park Road was upgraded for the opening of the Outer Circle bus route. It had originally been called Park Road, but the Harborne name was added in the nineteenth century in order to differentiate between it and other Park Roads in Birmingham. The section between Harborne High Street and Vivian Road was originally known as Poyners Lane, and was lined with terraces of mid-Victorian houses interspersed with older property, dating from the 1840s. The vacant site on the left, before the tall gabled house, is now occupied by a 1970s baptist church. On the right, in the slightly set-back building, is the only commercial premises in the block, which for many years was owned by A.E. Davis, a jobbing builder. Delivering milk to the houses on the left is a Midland Counties Dairy Morrison battery milk float, first registered in July 1953. (Birmingham Central Library)

Above: Until the early 1920s, Harborne Park Road was little more than a country lane, but it was rebuilt as a dual carriageway in 1926 in preparation for the opening of the new Outer Circle bus service. Travelling up Harborne Park Road towards Harborne and passing Bishops Croft, where the diocesan offices of the Bishop of Birmingham are to be found, is 2397 (JOJ 397), which was one of the final batch of thirty exposed-radiator Crossley-bodied Crossley DD42/7s that were delivered with the down-draught Crossley HOE7/5B engine. It is being overtaken by an Austin A40 Farina, a model that, although introduced in 1958, could justifiably claim to be the first true hatchback. (A.D. Broughall)

Above: The double-sided bench in the shade of mature trees lining the central reservation must have been an ideal place for relaxing, maybe reading a book. The spade leaning against the open gate suggests work of some kind was underway at 194 Harborne Park Road on this sunny day in 1961. Two years earlier, this address had been the home of the Harborne Riding School, then ironically owned for a short time by a Mr Thomas Sadler. (Birmingham Central Library)

Opposite below: Known as the Field House, the residence at 11 Harborne Park Road stands on the corner of St Mary's Road. The three-storey house was built mainly in the nineteenth century, with an earlier core dating from the previous century. The first- and second-floor outer windows are tripartite sash and the central first-floor window has a pointed interlaced arched head. The bay on the left-hand side with the small-paned dormer was added much later. It has been claimed that there was a Roman well in the rear garden. (Birmingham Central Library)

Above: The Golden Cross public house, seen here on the corner of Metchley Lane and Harborne Park Road, stands in almost exactly the same spot as the original red-brick pub of the same name. Today the Golden Cross, recently owned by Firkin and having undergone various name changes in recent times, has reverted to its original name. It is currently owned by Arena Pubs. The frontage now bears an electronic noticeboard for displaying various greeting messages on behalf of its patrons. (A. Spettigue)

Opposite below: What a difference seven years make! At the top of the hill at the Selly Oak end of Harborne Lane is Selly Oak Park, with the Victorian house on the left marking the entrance to the park. This was presented to the local authority by Mrs Gibbins in 1899 and is thirty-three acres in size. Travelling towards Harborne from Selly Oak on 19 September 1935 is AEC Regent 661, 467 (OV 4467). This Short-bodied bus dated from September 1931 and was to survive the Second World War with its original body until it was withdrawn in 1945. The bus is being overtaken by an Austin 10/4, which had been introduced during the same year. The large tree in the middle of the central reservation marks the original hedgerow of the old narrow lane and is the large tree in the centre of the previous picture. Plodding up the hill, delivering to the early 1930s semi-detached houses, is a delightful horse-drawn bread van. In the distance, above the bread van and the almost-new houses, can be seen the Golden Cross public house at the junction with Metchley Lane. (Birmingham Central Library)

Above: Harborne Lane, beyond the Dudley No.2 Canal, was a country lane until the turn of the twentieth century. A certain amount of urban development had taken place with the creation of a pavement on one side of the road illuminated by gas lamps, but by 30 January 1928, it had yet to be developed, despite the increased traffic on the road with the introduction of the Outer Circle route. On the left is Harborne Lane Wharf, with access to the ill-fated Dudley No.2 Canal, and beyond it are some Victorian houses, the furthest one serving as the gatehouse to Selly Oak Park, and further on is Reservoir Road. On the right are allotments, which survive today as a small garden centre. (Birmingham Central Library)

Above: The chimneys of Elliott's rolling mill stand starkly in the background in the year that Elliott's was taken over by I.M.I. The Dudley No.2 Canal was declared as fit for traffic on 28 May 1798, having been built to get barge traffic from the Black Country into Birmingham by another route other than the Birmingham Canal. The main problem of this important link between the Worcester and Birmingham Canal at Selly Oak and the Dudley Canal was that it needed to have a tunnel built beneath the high ground between Bartley Green and Halesowen. When completed as a legging tunnel, the Lapal Tunnel was 3,795 yards long, making it the fourth-longest canal tunnel in the country. Its principal use was to convey coal from the pits alongside the canal, as well as iron from Netherton and limestone from beneath Castle Hill and the Wren's Nest Hill in Dudley. It was built cheaply, using bricks of the poorest quality from the worst of the three brickworks in California. Within five years of opening it was in trouble and this continued throughout its life, with poorly-built masonry and collapsing sections causing long periods of closure. By 1917, at the height of the First World War, boats were unable to get through because of the collapse of about twenty yards of tunnel. Despite proposals for its repair, the canal was officially closed to traffic on 22 September 1926. On 10 July 1929, work was well underway in the rebuilding of the canal bridge and tow path on the redundant canal in Harborne Lane, in order to accommodate the increased traffic of the new Outer Circle bus route, rather than the barges. (Birmingham Central Library)

Opposite below: 1449 (FOP 449), a Guy Arab II with a five-cylinder Gardner 5LW engine and a Park Royal body, which entered service on 1 December 1944, stands in the shadow of the I.M.I.'s Elliott Works at the bus stop in Harborne Lane, opposite Selly Oak bus garage. When new, this 'utility' bus was fitted with wooden-slatted seating, which (to the relief of practically everyone) was removed during 1449's first overhaul, completed on 21 March 1946. The Corporation's policy was to replace the buses delivered during the Second World War, and despite looking in good condition here in 1948, not long after being allocated to Harborne garage for its last year in service, it was withdrawn on 31 December 1950 and was broken up the following June. Wartime buses were not regularly used on the No.11 service until 1948, and it is pictured travelling on the inner ring towards Selly Oak and Cotteridge. In the background is the crest of Harborne Bridge over the by now long closed Dudley No.2 Canal. (R.A. Mills)

Above: A late 1920s Rolls-Royce Phantom saloon turns out of Gibbins Road and onto the new canal bridge on 28 July 1931. Standing at the bus stop is an AEC 504 with an open staircase body built by Shorts of Rochester. 124 (OM 223) has just loaded up with its last gentleman passenger and is about to wend its way to Harborne on the No.11 route. On the left is the bus garage end of Selly Oak tram depot, which is being passed by the 1931 registered motorcycle combination owned by Edward Millward, carpenter and joiner, who was based in Reservoir Road. On the other side of Harborne Lane, beyond the silver-painted bollards with the ornate lighting, are a stern-looking bus driver and a mother holding her infant, waiting for the next bus. Behind them are the tall walls of the Elliott Works of Imperial Metal Industries. On the left is the still quite new Selly Oak depot and garage, which opened on 12 July 1927 to replace Bournbrook tram depot in Dawlish Road. It had a capacity for eighty tramcars, compared to the old C.B.T. premises, which only held forty-six trams. (Birmingham Central Library)

Above: From the bus stop opposite Selly Oak bus garage, the next stop – somewhat confusingly for the casual or occasional passenger on the No.11 route – was not at any of the bus stops alongside Graves' tool-making factory in Chapel Lane, but around the corner in Bristol Road. As the buses were frequently held up at the traffic lights before they turned right into Bristol Road, there was probably more unauthorised jumping off and jumping on buses at Selly Oak than at any other point on the No.11 route. A motorcyclist, a Standard 8 and a learner driving a Hillman Minx all conspire to hide the identity of the 2526 class Guy Arab III Special, which is standing between the Oak Cinema on the left and the Plough and Harrow public house at the traffic lights at the top of Chapel Lane and its junction with Bristol Road in around 1958. (J.H. Taylforth)

Right: The old oak tree was planted in about 1830 by John Rodway who was the owner of Selly Oak House. The oak tree grew on the corner of Bristol Road and Oak Tree Lane and survived until 1909, when it was felled in order to remove the sheer obstructive bulk of it – here it is seen in the year before this took place. Behind the tree on the corner of Harborne Lane and Bristol Road is the mid-Victorian Oak Inn, that for many years had the splendid hand-painted sign on its wall for Mitchells & Butlers Gold Medal Ales and Extra Stouts. In the distance, belching out a pall of smoke, is the chimney for part of W. Elliott & Sons metal works, which was in Chapel Lane. Elliott's provided much of the impetus for the growth of Selly Oak after 1853 and then became a world leader in the manufacture of sheathing metal which was used for plating ships. Opposite Elliott's factory was the White Horse Inn, which was closed only ten days before the Oak Inn as part of the same abysmal road scheme. (Birmingham Central Library)

Opposite below: Passing through Selly Oak on 7 June 1952, when working on the No.71 service to Rubery, is tramcar 796. It is a Brush-bodied E.M.B. air-brake tramcar which entered service in the last months of 1928. It is waiting outside the Oak Cinema, just off the photograph on the left, which opened in 1929 and closed in November 1979. This had been the original C.B.T. electric tram terminus, which in 1915 had been numbered thirty-five. On the right is St John's Methodist Church, standing on the corner of Elliott Road, which had been completed in 1876 and extended in 1908. It was demolished in the late 1970s as part of the road widening through Selly Oak, which also claimed the Plough and Harrow public house at the Chapel Lane junction with Bristol Road. This Ansell-owned pub dated from 1900, and was known for its first four years as the New Inn. Alongside this pub in Chapel Lane is a Bradford estate car, fitted with a flat twin 1005cc engine whose origins dated from 1913. It was a pretty, if old-fashioned little van derivative, with a top speed of 55mph transmitted through its three-speed synchromesh gearbox, but which would climb the side of a cliff. It was alongside where the Bradford is waiting that the No.11 bus service had to turn right into Bristol Road. Behind the tram, the Wolseley Hornet and the Morris Eight is the white-painted Dog and Partridge, which survived the road widening of 1987 but was closed by 1997. (R.B. Parr)

Above: Having turned left from Bristol Road into Oak Tree Lane, there was a bus stop outside the row of Victorian shops which stretched as far as Lottie Road. 2499 (JOJ 499), another one of Harborne garage's allocation of Crossley DD42/7s, waits to leave the stop on its way to Cotteridge on the No.11 route. Behind the bus (pictured in 1968, about a year before its withdrawal), roughly where the somewhat straggly tree is visible, was where the old oak stood until 1909. The public house in Bristol Road on the corner with Harborne Lane was the Oak Inn, which finally called time on 14 July 1983 to make way for a Sainsbury's supermarket and road widening. (M.R. Keeley).

Above: An aerial photograph of Selly Oak Hospital and surrounding area, 1926. From the bottom left-hand corner, Raddlebarn Road snakes its way past what had been Kings Norton Workhouse. The Woodland nurses homes are clearly visible, as are the cricket and football grounds and the geometric pattern of the allotments. The No.11 would drop (and still drops) those passengers bound for the hospital at Oak Tree Lane, which just skirts the bottom of the photo. (Birmingham Central Library)

Opposite below: On leaving Selly Oak, the No.11 route continues along Oak Tree Lane until it reaches Selly Oak Hospital on the corner of Raddlebarn Road. The largest part of the hospital was originally the Kings Norton Union Workhouse, whose foundation stone was laid on 21 August 1895. With the slightly later infirmary being built on the land between the Birmingham & West Suburban railway line and Raddlebarn Road, the two buildings comprised a total of twelve imposing brick-built two- and three-storey blocks, which still serve as the present-day core of Selly Oak Hospital. The top end of what is today known as Raddlebarn Road, at the Oak Tree Lane end, was originally known as Workhouse Lane but was tactfully renamed. The bus working on the No.11 route is 2986 (JOJ 986), which is a Guy Arab IV 6LW with a fifty-five seat Metro-Cammell body. It is passing the entrance to Raddlebarn Road, and behind the fingerpost sign is the 1960s out-patient part of the hospital. (D.R. Harvey Collection)

Above: Bournville Rest House is situated in the centre of the triangular green at Bournville Village. The Rest was modelled on an early seventeenth-century yarn market at Dunster in Somerset and dates from 1914. It was built to commemorate the silver wedding anniversary of Mr and Mrs Cadbury the previous year. The Rest, octagonal in design, has two tiers of windows, which are separated by over-hanging eaves. (Birmingham Central Library)

Opposite above: On a sunny day in around 1967, in the tree-lined Linden Road, 2636 (JOJ 636), a Daimler CVD6 with a Metro-Cammell body, passes Bournville Junior School on its way out of the valley of Bournbrook en route to Selly Oak, after reaching Woodbrooke Road and the Ruskin Institute at the top of the steepest part of the climb. The school was built in 1902 and contains a cupola with a world-famous carillon of forty-eight bells which are played at least once a week. The bus is one of a batch which entered service on 1 July 1951, introduced to replace the Coventry Road trolleybuses. (D.R. Harvey Collection)

Above: Hopefully, the cricket match in progress at Bournville would have gladdened the heart of George Cadbury, the founder of Cadbury's and a noted social reformer. Born in 1839 in Edgbaston, he aimed to improve the working lives of those he and his family employed in their chocolate and cocoa works in the city centre. In 1879, Cadbury acquired the site we now know as Bournville. Cadbury World, now as well known as the chocolate and Cadbury himself, provides sightseeing tours and information about the factory and one of Birmingham's most famous and favourite sons. (A. Spettigue)

Left: Kings Norton United Reform Church, where it once stood at the corner of Watford Road and Woodfall Road. Services were originally held in the chapel hall before the church was built in 1903. It was demolished in 1953. (Birmingham Central Library)

Above: An almost-new Crossley, 2324 (a DD42/7 with a Crossley H30/24R body of the earlier type including half-drop ventilators in the saloon windows), stands in Watford Road in 1951 outside the row of shops which date from the last decade of Queen Victoria's reign. It is working on the No.11 route on the anti-clockwise run and looks positively sparkling, with its dark blue varnished paintwork reflecting the road surface. All the saloon windows are open, as is the driver's windscreen, suggesting that it was a hot day as the bus pulls away from the shelters which it shared with the No.18 and No.23 services. On the right is a large newsagent advertising Clarke's Coaches, a company based in Rubery which was a well-known tour operator. Behind the bus shelter is Grainger's Ladies' Outfitters, who specialised in coats, skirts and dresses for the fashion-conscious. (A.B. Cross)

Opposite above: One of the first classes of new-look front buses to enter service were the Daimler CVD6s of the 2031 class, which had Metro-Cammell bodies that were very similar to those on the short-length Guy Arab III Specials. 2031 (JOJ 31) entered service on 20 September 1950, some three weeks in advance of the next bus of the class, but nine months after the previous exposed-radiator Daimler, 2030. The reason for this delay was the design changes necessary for both the chassis and the body in order to accommodate the re-styled front bonnet arrangement. By the time 2031 was in service, nearly all the new-look front Crossleys had been delivered and about twenty-two of the Guys. The Daimler rolls with the camber of Linden Road as it passes the junction with Bournville Lane where the sign on the left warns of the 10ft-high low bridge at Bournville Station. From Bournville Lane, where the single-decker-operated No.27 bus route went, emerges a two-tone painted Hillman Minx Series II. (R.F. Mack)

Above: 3398 (398 KOV) is parked in Watford Road at the same bus stop in Cotteridge as 2324 in the previous photograph some twenty-five years later. This Daimler Fleetline CRG6LX, with a Metro-Cammell body fitted with seventy-six seats, was more usually to be found working on the No.39 service to Witton or the No.33 to Kingstanding from its home base at Perry Barr garage. The B.C.T. Fleetlines were never regular performers on the Outer Circle until the final withdrawal of what came to be known as the 'Birmingham Standard', which roughly meant a rear entrance, open-back platform, half-cab double-decker. As the final day of operation was not until the last day of October 1977, the Birmingham Fleetlines themselves, by now in PTE ownership, were well past their first flush of use. (L. Mason)

Opposite below: The English Electric-bodied Daimler COG5, 1237 (FOF 237), stands at the bus stop in front of Barclay's Bank on 15 April 1950 when working on the No.11 route. Behind it, through the scaffolding of the shelter, is tram 840, built in 1928. This was one of the Short-bodied, Maley & Taunton bogie trams, which was standing at the terminal track stub of the No.36 route that was also outside its home Cotteridge depot. This bus entered service on 1 March 1940 and was unique, being the only new English Electric body to be mounted on a B.C.T. Daimler. The driver of 1237 will be hauling his charge hard to the right into Watford Road and off to Bournville and Selly Oak. This bus would outlive the tram by over two years, not being withdrawn until 4 September 1954. 1237's 'afterlife' was unusual as it was sold to Kallis Lefkaritis of Larnaca, Cyprus, where it was cut down into a single-decker and ran for at least another ten years. (J. Cull)

Above: An immaculately turned-out bus was considered in Birmingham to be the accepted norm, but occasionally the Transport Department excelled itself. In this case, in around 1958, an eleven-year-old bus turns into Watford Road, looking as though it has 'just come out of the box' – even its tyres are shining! It was less common to see a Daimler CVA6 working in the No.11 route than, for example, a Crossley or a Leyland, because with their small AEC 7.58 litre engines, there was always the suspicion that in the peak they were not quite up to the job, especially in keeping time. What was forgotten, however, was that with their Metro-Cammell bodies, they had only an unladen weight of 7 tons 12 cwt, which was not that poor as a power-to-weight ratio. 1554 (GOE 554), the penultimate member of these first seventy-five buses delivered after the Second World War, spent its first fourteen years at Harborne garage. (R.F. Mack)

Above: On its way into Cotteridge when travelling along Pershore Road, the No.11 route passed the old Cotteridge Police Station, which was donated to the Birmingham Constabulary in the early 1930s. It was a lovely house with a wood-panelled entrance hall, which might not have been appreciated by some of the 'guests' who entered the front door. 3123 (MOF 123), a 1953-built Daimler CVG6 with a Crossley H30/25R body, has just passed Francis Road and is going over the former Midland Railway's Lifford Curve line, having just passed Frances Road in around 1967. It is being followed by a Plaxton-bodied Ford coach. (R.F. Mack)

Above: Pershore Road took the No.11 bus route down an increasingly steep hill into Cotteridge. Looking towards Cotteridge on a dingy-looking day, you can see the hazy outline of St Agnes' Church tower visible in the distance. The horse and cart is passing across the railway bridge over the Lifford Curve on Pershore Road. On 30 May 1935, needless to say, there is neither a tram nor a bus in sight, but there is lots of fascinating detail, such as the advertisement for the well-known Birmingham Races, but also the long-forgotten Shirley Races. In the hoardings to the right of the tall chimney stacks of the Grant Arms public house, is another advert for King George V's Jubilee Trust, while parked in front of the row of shops on the right is a small Morris commercial delivery van. (Birmingham Central Library)

Opposite below: Cotteridge was a thriving shopping centre of Edwardian origin, with three churches, a school, a cinema, a wide range of shops and even its own tram depot. Dominating the scene is St Agnes' Church, which was built in the decorated style in 1902. With its large interior of brick and stone, as well as an impressive tower, was probably the best ecclesiastical piece of architecture in Cotteridge. Obviously, this was the one to be demolished and was replaced in the late 1990s by a supermarket! Outside the church is a row of trams, each waiting for their turn to get to the terminus. Between the church and the end of the gabled row of shops was the entrance to Cotteridge depot. It later became a bus garage, finally being closed on 25 October 1986 to be replaced by a private development of luxury flats, while St Agnes' Church was demolished in the early 1990s. The driver hastily returns to the cab of his year-old new-look front Crossley, 2493 (JOJ 493), in Pershore Road, Cotteridge in July 1951, while waiting to return to the city on the No.36 route was tramcar 832. It was from here that car 821 ran away in October 1942, when the brakes leaked off. (J.C. Gillham)

The steep climb over the Worcester & Birmingham Canal Bridge below the Breedon Cross public house, was where tram 821 turned over at the junction of Pershore Road with Fordhouse Lane in the early morning of 26 October 1942. The tram was left without its handbrake on outside Cotteridge depot and the air-brake leaked off, allowing the tramcar to run away down the hill towards the Breedon. It failed to take the 'S' bend by the pub and turned over at the bottom of the hill. The climb was undertaken by Outer Circle buses, which in wet weather must have been difficult having to cope with the combination of slippery steel rails and smooth cobbles, as it was on 5 January 1933 when a mother and her teenage daughter waited for a tram. The glory days for the Breedon Cross faded away in the 1970s, leaving it variously closed or derelict until an arson attack finished off the once-elegant façade in 2001. (Birmingham Central Library)

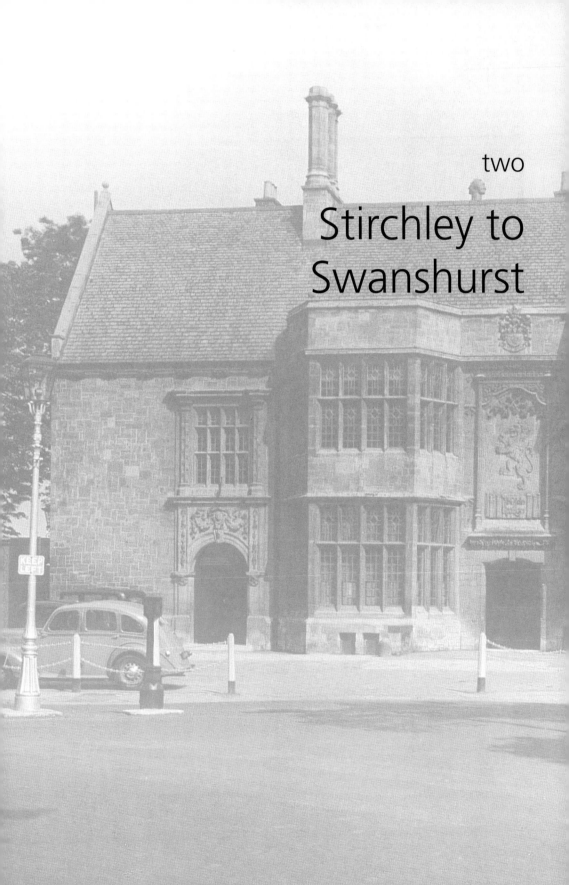

two

Stirchley to Swanshurst

Above: 2896 (JOJ 896), a Daimler CVG6 with a Crossley H30/25R body of 1953 vintage, is passing the old King's Norton Palace of Varieties in Pershore Road. The cinema opened in 1922 and it became the Savoy ten years later. The cinema closed on 2 February 1958 and it was subsequently converted into a factory which is still there today. 2896 has been repainted with the post-1962 black waist-rail fleet number. The bus has come down the hill from Cotteridge in Pershore Road and it will go over the awkward Breedon Bridge that carries the road over the Worcester & Birmingham Canal as it goes to Kings Heath. (R.F. Mack)

Opposite below: The tree-lined Fordhouse Lane ran across the quite deeply incised River Rea valley and 2533 (JOJ 533), a Guy Arab III Special with a 26ft-long Metro-Cammell H30/24R body, speeds across the comparatively flat flood plain on its way to Kings Heath. This bus eventually became the last Birmingham City Transport back-loader bus to operate on the No.11 route at the end of October 1977 and was subsequently bought for preservation. Travelling in the opposite direction towards Pershore Road is a Sunbeam Rapier Mark III, which is speeding past the Stirchley sign. In the distance, a twin rear-wheeled Ford Transit van approaches the Wilmot Breedon factory, which was located in the crook of the bend in Fordhouse Lane, just before the road climbed to the Breedon junction with Pershore Road. Wilmot Breedon made car accessories mainly for the B.M.C. Group at Longbridge, where anything from chromed door handles, locks, ignition keys, bumpers or dashboard assemblies might be supplied to the nearby Austin. (R.F. Mack)

Above: Displaying an old destination blind which also shows the route number, new-look front Crossley DD42/7 (with a Crossley H30/24R body), 2429 (JOJ 429), turns out of Fordhouse Lane into Pershore Road in around 1967, which was the year before it was withdrawn. Drivers of Crossleys had to be particularly careful at this point as the Crossleys had manual synchromesh gearboxes and from a standing start in Fordhouse Lane, it was necessary to get into second gear with a 'snap' gear change before climbing the steep rise up to Lifford Lane, the Breedon Cross pub and Breedon Bridge. The newsagent's shop in the background is where tram 821's top deck finished after the unfortunate vehicle had run away without anyone on it from the Cotteridge in 1942. (R.F. Mack)

Hancock's Garage was owned in 1957 by J. and A. Hancock, motor car engineers. The signs hanging outside show that the garage was an agent for BP and Shell. Summer shows are advertised outside the garage and top of the bill was the Arena Theatre, who were playing a summer season at Cannon Hill Park. (Birmingham Central Library)

A very different era – Fordhouse Lane, pictured in one of the never-ending Edwardian summers, in around 1910. Only the brook running across the lane gives any indication today of the exact location of the photograph. (Birmingham Central Library)

Standing in the shadow of the Church of St Mary Magdalen on 7 October 1930, on the recently rebuilt and widened Pineapple Bridge, is an AEC 504 with a Short H26/26RO body. 167 (ON 1318) entered service on 7 December 1925, just a few months before the opening of the completed Outer Circle bus route. To the modern eye, these buses look antiquated and, indeed, such was the pace of bus chassis development that they would become obsolete before their time. Yet they revolutionised the bus services in the city, to the extent that by the time the last of the five-series family had been delivered in March 1929, the writing was on the wall for the trams, as these outside staircase buses had proved that buses could do better the job that had previously been done by tramcars. With their 6.8 litre petrol engines, buses like these opened up the new housing estates being built around the city, many of the houses looking very much like those incorporated into the row of shops to the right of the bus on the corner of Allens Croft Road and Millbrook Road. (Birmingham Central Library)

Climbing up the hill from Fordhouse Lane and crossing Pineapple Bridge on its way into Vicarage Road is 3063 (MOF 63). This bus was the first of the MOF-registered Guy Arab IVs to enter service in January 1954, though the protracted delivery of these 100 M.C.C.W.-bodied buses took some seventeen months to complete. In around 1958, 3063, one of Harborne's small batch of Arab IVs, pulls away from the stop that was located on the bridge over the old Midland Railway Camp Hill railway line. Until 27 January 1941, this line had regular commuter traffic on it, serving stations at Brighton Road, Moseley, Kings Heath, Hazelwell (which was just beyond the next bridge up the line towards Birmingham) and Lifford, although the latter closed on the last day of September 1940. There seemed to be an almost sadistic delight taken by the traffic planners in placing bus stops in the most awkward places, and Pineapple Bridge was an excellent example of this skill, which seemed designed to irritate the driving staff. (A.B. Cross)

The first pre-fabs were put up in Birmingham in 1945 and, in all, 4,625 were built on land which was not designated for future housing construction. Boasting a large living room, a built-in kitchen, two bedrooms and a bathroom and toilet, when first occupied they must have seemed like the lap of luxury, but by the late 1950s many of them, including the ones seen here on the right in Vicarage Road, were getting towards the end of what was only ever intended to be a short life-span. A four-wheel Morrison Electricar DV4 dustcart, dating from around the outbreak of the war, is doing its rounds in the distance in Vicarage Road on the No.11 bus route on 29 April 1959. Between July 1918, when a 2½ ton Edison was purchased, and January 1971, Birmingham City Salvage Department operated 262 battery-electric dustcarts, with a maximum fleet strength of 157 vehicles being achieved in the second year of the Second World War. These dustcarts were to be found quietly 'pootling' about throughout the city as they collected refuse, or, as it was referred to in the Department, 'salvage'. The battery-electrics collected in excess of ninety-five per cent of the city's rubbish, which was then taken to the vehicles' homebase that was also an incineration plant. This 4-tonner was based at the nearby Lifford depot, and as it is opposite Priory Road and approaching the Rectory for St Mary Magdalen, it is at the right end of Vicarage Road to get home on low batteries, though the climb up the canal bridge at the Breedon Cross might occasionally catch it out. (Birmingham City Engineers and Surveyors Department)

The parade of shops on the right, set back from the carriageway in Vicarage Road between Cartland Road and Priory Road, dates from the 1920s, while the Victorian ones opposite went up to the Kings Road junction. Making a rare appearance on the Outer Circle bus route is one of Acocks Green garage's AEC Regent III RT-types. 1633 (GOE 633) had a four-bay construction body built by Park Royal and was one of the replacement 1947 deliveries for an order which, but for the unavailability of new buses in 1941, would have launched AEC's star once more in Birmingham. However, it was not to be and seven years later, fifteen of these unusually styled buses appeared. Although London Transport had over 4,800 RTs, in Birmingham they were not popular as they had air-brakes and air-controlled gearboxes. Thus they could only be driven by Acocks Green drivers who had been 'passed out' on them. With their strange bodies which combined rather uncomfortably the best (or worst) of B.C.T. and London Transport practice, the buses had non-standard staircases and a seating layout which was 'different' from the standard Birmingham bus. Their appearance was not helped by the frontal aspect's combination of tall, gaunt windscreen, low bonnet line and headlights which were at different heights. As a result of all these factors, the RTs were hardly ever seen on the Circle and even when they were, they were only used on half-turns and never all the way round the No.11 route. (A.B. Cross)

The Red Lion public house, designed by Mitchells & Butlers house architect C.E. Bateman, opened on 11 August 1904. This building was a pioneering pub, heavily influenced by the Arts and Crafts movement of William Morris, with overtones of the Art Nouveau style. The concept was to create a country inn within the city that evoked an earlier age. The Red Lion has two massive two-storey bays with leaded windows and is faced with a red Wildon stone. It was built on land owned by the Cartland family, whose fortune was built on a brass-making foundry near Broad Street. They had built cottage-style houses at the edge of Kings Heath, so the family approved of their local inn being built in the 'Merrie England' style. Parked in the pub's car park is a 1937 Standard Flying Ten, and on the extreme left is another Standard, this time a 1935 Sixteen model. (Birmingham Central Library)

Above: Speeding along Vicarage Road into Kings Heath is 1050 (CVP 150), a Daimler COG5 with Metro-Cammell H30/24R body which entered service on 1 August 1937, passing the row of Victorian houses and the junction with Highbury Road on the right. Between 1 September 1957 and September 1958, three bus services were taken over from Midland Red in the Walsall Road and College Road areas. As a result the Corporation required more vehicles, so forty-two pre-war buses were taken out of storage or transferred from the snowplough fleet and prepared for service. Forty-one of them were placed in service after having received a mechanical overhaul and a touch-up and varnish, with the first, 1082, re-entering service in June 1957. 1050 was one of the buses brought back into service in 1957, lasting until May 1960, although appearances of these elderly vehicles on the Circle became increasingly rare as they began to show their age … but what an Indian summer! (R.F. Mack)

Above: The Kings Heath end of Vicarage Road is lined by late Victorian housing which were basically just a continuation of the village. Travelling away from Kings Heath in Vicarage Road on a 'service extra' in 1958, having just left the bus shelter near All Saint's Road, is 1129. Initially allocated to Yardley Wood garage when it was returned into service in 1958 as their solitary Daimler, COG5 1129 (CVP 229), fitted in 1948 with the M.C.C.W. body from 1072, is working towards Cotteridge in 1959. 1129 entered service on 15 November 1937 and survived until 31 May 1960. These pre-war buses were powered by a five-cylinder Gardner engine, which when coupled with the lightweight bodywork weighing around 6 tons 16 cwt, produced a power-to-weight ratio that made their performance very similar to a post-war Daimler CVG6 of the type seen in the companion volume *The Inner Circle*. (R.F. Mack)

Opposite above: One of the ten pre-production Daimler Fleetline CRG6LXs of 1962, 3247 (247 DOC), is travelling along Vicarage Road on a short-working back to Perry Barr. The trees of Kings Heath Park are to its offside, behind which used to lie the site of The Priory. This grand early nineteenth century house had a huge conservatory attached to it and was a centre for many social events amongst the influential Victorians of Birmingham. The house had been the home latterly of the unmarried John Howard Cartland, until his death in 1940, whose family of brass-founders are remembered in the nearby Cartland Road. The house was demolished in 1956 and the bus is passing the old entrance drive to the replacement King Edward VI School Camp Hill which occupies the site today. On the right is the entrance to Colmore Road with its mixture of turn-of-the-twentieth-century villas and mid-1920s semi-detached houses. (D.R. Harvey Collection)

Above: All Saint's Parish Church stands on the impressive corner site where Vicarage Road and High Street, Kings Heath, meet. The Parish Church was designed by F. Preedy and was first consecrated in 1859; the church was extended with a chancel and a south-west tower with a spire in 1899, but was built to a budget – which shows in the poor quality of the architectural detail. Since the removal of the underground public lavatories which were to the left of the bus, the failings of the building have been negated by the improved urban environment. One of the 1937 Daimler COG5s brought back into service in 1958 was 1115 (CVP 215), which had received another Metro-Cammell H30/24R body from 1083 in March 1948. These elderly Daimlers had been held in store as a reserve fleet and on re-entry into service, they were scattered around the garages. 1115 (CVP 215) was allocated to Perry Barr garage and was somewhat surprisingly allowed out on all-day service on the Outer Circle route, here seen turning into Alcester Road in 1959. (A.B. Cross)

Opposite below: Turning into Addison Road from Alcester Road on a short-working back to Acocks Green garage, is what at first sight looks like a normal new-look front Guy Arab IV bus. In fact, nothing could be further from the truth! 3001 (LOG 301) had a lightweight Saunders-Roe fifty-five seat body which, at an all-up weight of 7 tons 4½ cwt, made this bus some sixteen hundredweight lighter than a standard Metro-Cammell Guy 27-footer. The chassis, having appeared at the 1952 Commercial Motor Show, was originally equipped with a Gardner 6LW engine, but in 1953, some five years earlier, it was fitted with a smaller 7.0 litre Garner 5LW engine. The bus operated for the whole of its twenty-year life from Acocks Green garage. (A.B. Cross)

Above: The No.11 route turned out of Vicarage Road and went along Alcester Road for about 200 yards before turning into Addison Road. This section of road in Kings Heath was little more than an extension of High Street, and as such is one of the most prosperous and important suburban shopping centres in the city. It was developed during the 1870s, although this top end by All Saints Church dates from the Edwardian period. In around 1956, making a rare excursion from Hockley garage, is 1801 (HOV 801), a Daimler CVD6 with a M.C.C.W. body of 1948, working on the inner ring of the Outer Circle route. It is being followed by a Morris Eight Series I. (J.H. Taylforth)

Above: This view of 180 Addison Road in 1958 was taken because the owner, William Millward, was seeking permission to put up a sign advertising his painting and decorating business. Most of the houses in this narrow street are terraced and at this date provide a fine display of Art Deco style stained-glass windows. Sadly, many of these have now been replaced. (Birmingham Central Library)

Above: After 1986, the Outer Circle stopped using Coldbath Road because it was deemed to be too narrow, and the adverse camber into Swanshurst Lane was always a struggle for drivers, even after the introduction of power steering. So, the new route was diverted along Brook Lane to the fire station on the corner of Yardley Wood Road, where the No.11 buses turned left and ran along the western side of Swanshurst Park before regaining the old route into Swanshurst Lane once more. On 20 September 1959, the open space in front of the pre-war houses in Brook Lane alongside Swanshurst Girls' School was intended for a dual carriageway, which was (along with other roads which started being built immediately before the war) not completed for another thirty years. (Birmingham City Engineers & Surveyors Dept)

Opposite below: Some of the first buses to operate on the new Outer Circle route when it was finally finished on 7 April 1926 were these A.D.C. 507s with outside staircase Buckingham fifty-two seater bodies. John Buckingham's coach-builders factory was in Bradford Street and they were beginning to get a good reputation among local bus and coach operators. They unfortunately succumbed to the Depression, having successfully tendered to body the eleven Leyland TB1 trolleybuses for the Nechells route, but this had to be given up and the order was transferred to Short Brothers, who were bodying a batch of AEC Regents for B.C.T. at the time. 272 (OX 1548), which entered service on 26 September 1927, is still on rubber tyres as it turns from Coldbath Road into Brook Lane at the Billesley public house. This mock-Elizabethan roadside public house had replaced a much smaller late eighteenth-century building in 1927, the same year as the bus entered service. (Commercial Postcard)

On the corner of Brook Lane and Wheelers Lane, the Billesley Arms has been a noted landmark in the Kings Heath district for generations. Originally known as the Billesley Arms, it has also been called the Billesley Hotel, the New Billesley Hotel and the Billesley. (Birmingham Central Library)

The first post-war buses to be delivered to Birmingham arrived in 1947, comprising seventy-five Daimler CVA6s with a unique style of Birmingham body, which had many of the design features of later deliveries coupled with a very thin body pillar design. 1524 (GOE 524) heels over as it turns into Swanshurst Lane after crossing Yardley Wood Road on 20 September 1963. In the background are some pre-fabs built in the late 1940s, forming a row along one side of Yardley Wood Road. Although they were to have a life expectancy of ten years, many pre-fabs survived for over twenty years, including those in Coldbath Road, while in nearby Wake Green Road, the last seventeen in Birmingham have been modernised and preserved. Many buses of this class had been withdrawn when their fitness certificates were due for renewal in December 1961, yet six of them soldiered on until July 1966. At this time, 1524 was still working from Harborne garage, but by early 1965 it had been transferred to Birchfield Road garage, which was known as the 'home for the elderly'. (D.R. Harvey Collection)

A Metro-Cammell-bodied Daimler Fleetline CRG6LX, 3569 (BON 569C), stands at the outer ring clocking in at Bundy Clock in Swanshurst Lane, alongside Swanshurst Park. This batch of Fleetlines was the first complete delivery from Metro-Cammell to have the more attractive large 'V'-shaped windscreen than the earlier 'plain' box designs. In Birmingham, this style of front had been introduced on the Corporation's buses numbered 3391–3400, which had arrived during the previous year and had initially been developed at the request of Manchester CTD. (J.C. Walker)

The boating lake in Swanshurst Park in 1935. The park was opened in 1919 and its forty-four acres contain a delightful boating lake. For many years, it had an eighteen-hole miniature golf course, whose most peculiar feature was at the ninth tee, where the ground was obviously very near to the watertable as the whole area always seemed to bounce. (Birmingham Central Library)

The original mill at Sarehole dates from 1542. The current mill was built during the late eighteenth century and closed around 1919. It was restored in the late 1960s, mainly due to an appeal from members of the public. J.R.R. Tolkien, of *Lord of the Rings* fame, spent part of his boyhood in nearby Wake Green Road and later became involved in the public appeal to restore the mill. Tolkien himself may not have travelled on the No.11 bus, but it's certain that many thousands of his readers have. (Birmingham Central Library)

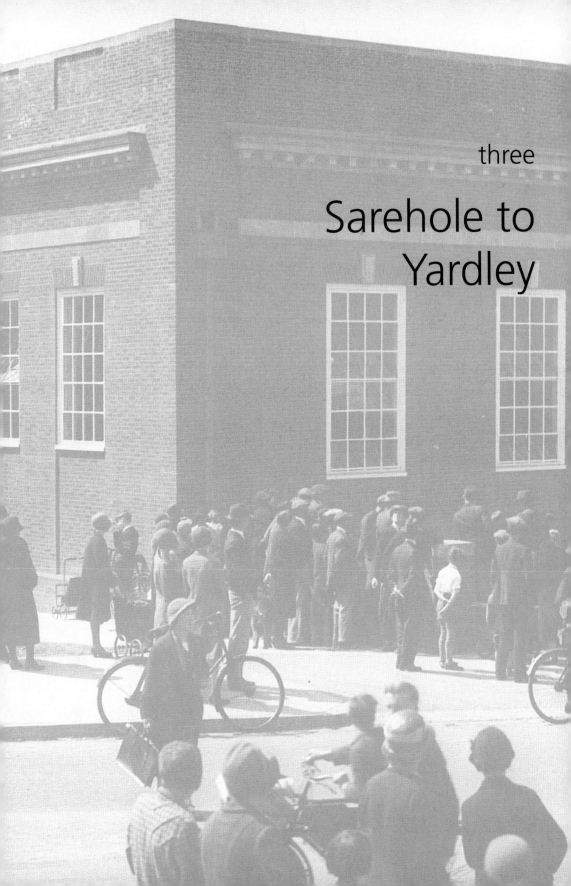

three

Sarehole to Yardley

Above: Although Cotteridge garage was on the Outer Circle, it usually did not provide any buses for the service. The exceptions were 'change buses', where a bus from another garage was deemed to be faulty and replaced at Cotteridge with one of their own. 1564 (GOE 564) – one of Cotteridge's – a 1947 Daimler CVG6 with an M.C.C.W. H30/24R body, which entered service on 1 November 1947, stands at the inner, anti-clockwise Bundy Clock on the River Cole Bridge just beyond Sarehole Mill in 1963. The bus was withdrawn in December 1964. Every route, including the Outer Circle, had Bundy Clocks, where the drivers had to 'peg the clock' in order to run to the timetable. It was a disciplinary offence to run early; lateness caused by traffic congestion or an accident could always be corrected by an inspector. (D.R. Harvey Collection)

Opposite above: In 1922, Cole Bank Lane had only recently been renamed Cole Bank Road and still had the rural feel that its old name implied. On the right is Sarehole Mill, which had been built in 1773 as one of sixteen mills on the River Cole. Many were built as grist mills, but were adapted to industrial purposes, making needles, wire, paper, edge-tools and rifle barrels. Sarehole was basically a corn mill, but had been converted to use steam during the period when it was used as an industrial centre (hence the chimney) to augment the somewhat variable water power. Alas, this was to change all too soon as the creeping suburbanisation of the 1920s began. Just to the right of the large tree and next to the brick parapet of the River Cole Bridge are three trilby-hatted men, two of whom are referring to a map, while between them are, stuck into the ground like javelins, three surveyor's ranging poles. The end of the rural idyll was in sight. (Birmingham Central Library)

Opposite below: The recently widened Colebank Road, across the River Cole valley floor, was one of the last schemes on the outer ring road not to be built to dual-carriageway standard. On Thursday 10 October 1935, a Metro-Cammell-bodied Daimler COG5, 739 (AOP 739), which had only entered service three months earlier, on 1 July, approaches the bus stop at Sarehole Mill on an Outer Circle working. On the right is the mill's chimney, which was unusual for a water mill, although Sarehole Mill, along with Titterford Mill, was partly converted to steam power which quadrupled its power output. (Birmingham Central Library)

Above: After leaving the River Cole valley, Cole Bank Road climbs steeply up to its junction with Stratford Road. 467 (OV 4467) approaches the newly-installed traffic island at Sarehole Road on 10 October 1935. This AEC Regent 661 was fitted with a Short Brothers H27/21R body, which was built in 1931 and had an upper saloon that did not extend completely over the cab; this was called 'the piano front', as it looked like the keyboard lid on an old upright. The semi-detached houses were built on farmland during the latter half of the 1920s and after just fourteen years, only the land on the Cole flood plain was left as parkland. Travelling in the opposite direction is a small petrol tanker, while parked facing up the hill is a 1935 Standard Twelve model, which cost £245 if it had the luxury of an optional Philco radio. (Birmingham Central Library)

Opposite below: The North Warwickshire railway line gave people living in Earlswood, Henley-in-Arden and Stratford the opportunity to commute to the newly-opened Moor Street Station. Looking out of the city at track level towards the next station at Yardley Wood in the late 1920s, reveals a neatly presented station with the majority of its facilities on the up-line platform: a cloakroom, a booking office, a waiting room, a ladies' waiting room and a gentlemen's lavatory. Beyond the passenger bridge is the road bridge on Stratford Road; the second bridge is the one in Sarehole Road which was crossed by the Outer Circle route. (Commercial Postcard)

Above: The Great Western Railway opened its North Warwickshire line to Bearley Junction on 1 July 1908 and the second station on the line was the one at Hall Green. By the time the Hall Green suburb had been completed, the increase in traffic necessitated the widening of the road bridge just to the south-west of the station over Cole Bank Road. Working on a football special to Villa Park is 430 (OG 430), which was an AEC Regent 661 with a forty-eight seater Vulcan body, built in Southport. Aston Villa were playing Barnsley and the Villa beat them 4-2 in front of a crowd of 38,000, with two goals from Frankie Broome and a goal apiece from Dai Astley and Eric Houghton. Happy days! (Birmingham Central Library)

Above: This is the old Hall Green garage whose premises stood in Stratford Road between Cole Bank Road and the corner of Green Road. The garage had a Ford dealership, which also included the American Lincoln marque and Fordson tractors. The car parked at the front of the shop is a Birmingham-registered Ford Model T, which was built at Trafford Park, Manchester, in 1920. In the distance, beyond Cateswell Road on the left, is a top-covered, open-vestibuled tram of the 71 class, which is working on a No.17 or No.18 route out of the city to Highfield Road, Hall Green. It is at the junction of Cole Bank Road and School Road, where the Outer Circle bus route crossed Stratford Road. (Birmingham Central Library)

Above: Fox Hollies Road was converted into a dual carriageway in 1929 as part of the scheme to build an outer ring road around the city. A 1925 Short-bodied AEC 504, by now on pneumatic tyres, speeds along Fox Hollies Road towards School Road when it was around six years old and the neat rows of semi-detached houses were perhaps only two or so years old. The bus, 164 (ON 1315), had an outside staircase as well as having an open driver's cab. Strangely, the first buses with enclosed cabs, which were slightly later versions of the 504 model, were not liked by the drivers. Apparently, the windscreen would steam up in the rain, making driving conditions difficult; many drivers preferred to pull down the rain shield/sun visor and put on their tarpaulin capes when it was pouring with rain. Travelling in the opposite direction along an otherwise deserted road is a Somerset-registered Austin Sixteen of 1927. (Birmingham Central Library)

Opposite below: The Church of the Ascension is on the corner of School Road and Fox Hollies Road. It was built in 1704 and was originally named Marston Chapel after Job Marston, a local landowner, who bequeathed the land and £2,200 for the building and landscaping of the site. The Worcestershire-based families of Marston, Greswolde, Este and Folliott owned land from Hall Green through Acocks Green and into Yardley at various points from medieval times up until the early twentieth century. If anyone was educated at Yardley Grammar School in Tyseley, then they would recognise these names as those of the school's four houses. The chapel was designed by one Sir William Wilson in the rare English Baroque style in brick with stone dressings consisting of a nave and a tower. A similar (though slightly more simply-styled) chancel and transepts were added in 1860, proving that Victorians were capable of architectural restraint. It became Hall Green Parish Church in 1907 and remains as one of the architectural gems on the Outer Circle bus route. (A. Spettigue)

Above: On a hot June day in 1959, Crossley-bodied Crossley DD42/7, 2417 (JOJ 417), stands at the stop at the corner of Olton Boulevard East outside the village paper shop in the shade of the mature lime trees. The driver, who is in his khaki summer uniform, is taking a short break as the queue of ladies shuffles forward to board this Harborne-allocated bus. 2417 was one of the last buses delivered to B.C.T. with an exposed radiator. Although they had the later, more powerful, down-draught HOE7/5B 8.6 litre Crossley engine, these buses were generally more difficult to drive than the contemporary Daimlers or Guys as they had manual synchromesh gearboxes, which meant that they 'had to be driven', making Crossleys harder work on hot summer days like this one. (D.F. Parker)

Above: Westley Road, looking towards Acocks Green, is viewed from outside Acocks Green bus garage on 18 March 1931. The tall building beyond the recreation park is on the corner of Broad Road. Although the view is pretty much recognisable today, the buildings (including the ones in the recreation ground) have long disappeared. (Birmingham Central Library)

Opposite below: Some of the inter-war building and rebuilding which took place in Birmingham's suburbs was extremely well planned, but it was a pity that so little rebuilding was done in the inner areas to get rid of the 40,000 unsanitary back-to-back houses, which would survive until the 1960s in some areas as shown in the companion volume *The Inner Circle*. Although Fox Hollies Road had been converted into a dual carriageway in 1931, it was part of only thirty miles of dual carriageway which had been built in the city by the outbreak of war. At the same time, one third of Birmingham's citizens lived in areas in the outer ring which had green grass, side verges and a housing density rate of barely fourteen to the acre. It couldn't last as the inter-war developments were extremely wasteful of land, but it did create a pleasant suburbia, through which, in the late 1940s, a 1946 Morris Eight Series E overtakes 1187 (FOF 187), a Daimler COG5 with a M.C.C.W. H30/24R body, which entered service in 1939. The bus has left the Olton Boulevard East junction and is travelling towards Stratford Road. (Birmingham Central Library)

Above: One of the three places where bus crews used to change was outside the recreation ground at the top of Westley Road, opposite Acocks Green bus garage. One of that garage's long-serving short-length, 26ft-long Metro-Cammell-bodied Guy Arab III Specials, 2574 (JOJ 574), sits awaiting a replacement driver, while the passengers contemplate the slides and the roundabout in the adjacent playground, perhaps wondering why they are not going 'round about' the Outer Circle a little more quickly. Drivers on the Circle would usually do two trips around the route (which was scheduled for two hours ten minutes per lap) before taking a break, although in addition to the three clocking-in points at the Bundy Clocks on each of the inner and outer rings, there were also designated points on the driver's timetable, (in the days before running cards), which were marked as SPs. These were smoking points, which although well-deserved, could be extremely frustrating for the paying public. (D.R. Harvey Collection)

Above: In 1909, one of Yardley Rural District Council's last acts through the finances of Worcestershire County Council was to build an elementary school for children between the ages of five and fourteen. There were three departments – for infants, boys and girls – and the school had the capacity for 1,198 pupils. It was built in a pleasing Arts and Crafts style and occupied a large site between Warwick Road and Westley Road. Just leaving the bus stop in Westley Road – hardly worthy of the title 'shelter' – is 2620 (JOJ 620), a Guy Arab III Special on 24 June 1969. This was only a few months before the Corporation gave up its municipal bus operations to the Labour Government-inspired West Midlands PTE. (A. Yates)

Opposite below: Westley Road, Acocks Green, 1932. A distant outside staircase A.D.C.507 double-decker, 306 (VP 1170), runs down the hill in Westley Road towards Acocks Green village on 8 September 1932. It is working on an inner ring Outer Circle timetable. Standing in the centre of the village, in the newly-reconstructed terminus area, is an ex-C.B.T. four-wheeler tramcar. Westley Road had previously been named Well Lane and had links to a tiny settlement which drew both its name and its water from Westley Brook, a tiny stream which was culverted in the 1790s when the nearby Warwick & Birmingham Canal was completed. The No.11 route was introduced between Six Ways, Erdington and Acocks Green on 15 January 1923 and was extended via Westley Road, Shaftesmoor Lane, College Road and Wake Green Road into Moseley Village on 14 May 1923. This covered the outer section of the No.1 route. It would take another three years before the Acocks Green to Moseley section became the No.1A route, taking a circuitous path into the city centre by way of Edgbaston. The true Outer Circle from the Kings Head, by way of Harborne, Cotteridge and Kings Heath, became a reality as the final piece of the 'jigsaw' on 7 April 1926. (Birmingham Central Library)

When Barford Street garage closed in 1954, most of its buses were transferred to the new Lea Hall garage, but Quinton garage received seven of Barford Street's GOE-registered Daimler CVG6s. As Quinton usually only had no more than two turns on the No.11 service, to see one of these buses on the Outer Circle was quite rare. A Standard Vanguard Phase 1 swings around the island in Warwick Road, as 1622 (GOE 622) stops outside the lavatories between the New Inns and the Warwick Cinema in Westley Road. This Metro-Cammell-bodied fifty-four seater, dating from 1948, is working on the No.11 service in 1955. (M.J. Dryhurst)

An AEC 504 of 1925 vintage is working on a football special, presumably to Villa Park, and is coming into Acocks Green village along Westley Road, having just passed the school buildings, which by this time were being administered by Birmingham Education Department. It is Monday 13 April 1931 – a time when Acocks Green was undergoing a period of considerable change. Just visible above the trees on the left is the roof of the Warwick Cinema, which opened in 1929, while the tram lines overhead and tracks show that the No.44 route was still at its first village terminus. On the right is the original New Inn, an Ansells-owned pub whose landlord at the time was a certain Howard Hemmings. This was the last year in which this building would trade as it was pulled down soon afterwards. It was replaced in 1934 by another pub called New Inn, a large, typical suburban public house, built where the hoardings for Empire Products and the concrete telephone box are located. The vacant land behind the car carrying wooden planks would soon be developed into a row of shops which curve around the corner from Westley Road into Warwick Road. (Birmingham Central Library)

The opening of Acocks Green Library on 14 June 1932. The ceremony had been performed earler in the day by the Lord Mayor, Alderman J.B. Burman. It was hailed as the largest branch libray in the city with a collection of 25,000 books. These volumes had been collected over the three preceding years by the librarian in charge, Mr H. Goodall, and had been stored in another library. The library comprised an adult reading room, junior room, newspaper room, reference room and staff workroom. The modern interior had the then new style open access system, allowing readers to choose their own books. Both the architects – Messrs John Osborne & Sons – and the builders – Mr J. Emlyn Williams – were local. (Birmingham Central Library)

The road layout of Acocks Green village was rebuilt in 1932, which resulted in the No.44 tram route getting its fourth terminus, in this case in the centre of the large traffic island. Waiting at the tram shelter is car 451. This was one of a pair of bogie cars taken over from the C.B.T. company in 1912, where it had been numbered 178. They were the longest trams in the fleet at 34ft 8in, had a seating capacity of sixty-six and were the only trams in the fleet to have five-side saloon windows. On 10 October 1932, an open-cab A.D.C. 507 turns out of Dudley Park Road on the No.11 service and will make its way through the somewhat strange road layout before turning into Westley Road on the left. The empty corner site in front of the city-bound Midland Red single-decker was where the old New Inn had been. It was demolished in 1931 and replaced by the new premises, built next to where the bus on the left is parked. The bus is one of the first batch in Birmingham to have enclosed staircases and cabs. It is 366 (OF 3998), which was bodied by Brush and is working on the No.1 route. (Birmingham Central Library)

Above: Sherborne Road, Acocks Green, from the railway station. The coming of the railway always brought people, and those people needed somewhere to live. When Acocks Green Station was opened by the Great Western Railway in 1852, superior properties, in the form of villa-type houses, large detached houses (such as the one on the right) and tall, three-storey terraces (such as those on the left) appeared within a few years. The housing developments in Sherborne Road and in the distant Dudley Park Road enabled the wealthier members of the new Victorian middle classes to commute into the centre of Birmingham in less than twenty minutes but remain living in what was still countryside. Even by the turn of the century, there were still seven farms in the Acocks Green area. By the time that this Edwardian scene was photographed, the railway station had been rebuilt (in 1906) and the smaller tunnel-back housing had been constructed on the northern side of the railway line in Douglas, Alexander and Florence Roads. (Birmingham Central Library)

Opposite above: Acocks Green Railway Station in Sherborne Road was originally opened in 1852 and was renamed Acocks Green and South Yardley in October 1878. The first station buildings were replaced with the present structure in 1906, with two canopied island platforms, while a few doors away – alongside The Avenue – was the Great Western Hotel. In the last days of steam-hauled trains, the glory days of the old Great Western Railway's main line between Paddington (London), Birmingham (Snow Hill) and Wolverhampton had been replaced by a tatty grandeur, with old-fashioned, traditional railwaymen swallowing their pride in trying to sustain services with increasingly under-maintained locomotives and stock. Chronic under-investment from central government led to the deliberate running down of services, the infamous Beeching Plan and at suburban stations like Acocks Green and South Yardley, a desperate need for a lick of paint. In around 1964, a north-bound express from the South Coast storms through the station, but it is being hauled by an ex-LMS Black Five 4-6-0, rather than one of the traditional GWR 4-6-0s. (A.W.V. Mace)

Above: Travelling along Yardley Road and about to pass the Augusta Road junction on the left is 109 (OM 208), one of the original batch of Short H26/26RO-bodied AEC 504s. By this time, the bus was equipped with pneumatic tyres, but originally ran with rubber tyres. This ten-year-old double-decker had just passed the Swan on this Wednesday morning. It is 13 June 1934 and business looks promising for Henry Ireland's fruiter's and greengrocer's shop, whose wooden trellises have a protective, if slightly sagging, canvas covering. Early on this bright summer's day, Megson (confectioner's) has two signs placed on his shop's forecourt for what might have been a welcome Lyons ice-cream. (Birmingham Central Library)

Above: Yardley Cemetery was opened in 1883 by Yardley RDC. In 1911, in accordance with the Greater Birmngham Act of the same year, Yardley Parish became part of Birmingham and the cemetery was acquired by Birmingham Corporation. Subsequently, a contract was drawn up between Birmingham Corporation and Yardley Parish agreeing reduced burial fees for residents of the old Yardley Parish. The original eight-acre graveyard has been extended considerably in recent times. In 1934, a second chapel was built, having been designed by Birmingham architect J.A. Swan. This was in addition to the original chapel and other buildings – such as offices, registrar's house and entrance gates – all of which had cost around £8,000. (Birmingham Central Library)

Above: The South Yardley Library was built almost next door to the Swan Hotel in Yardley Road. It was opened on 15 March 1939 and was an example of the attractive, yet plain and functional, brick-built structures which were being built elsewhere in the city in suburbs such as Acocks Green, Yardley Wood and Perry Common. The Lord and Lady Mayoress of Birmingham walk towards the entrance of the new library, while behind them is Yardley Road, with its small cluster of late 1920s council houses which were built in the shadows of the old C.B.T. tram depot. (Birmingham Central Library)

Opposite above: Crossing the Warwick & Birmingham Canal in Yardley Road on 18 August 1939, with Dalston Road on the left, is a 1935 Daimler COG5, working on an anti-clockwise Outer Circle duty. The bus is 772 (AOP 772), which was bodied by the Corporation's second bus body builder, the Birmingham Railway Carriage & Wagon Company. Their bodies could be easily identified from the more common Metro-Cammell ones by their rear-platform canopies having a deeper, but shallower, radius next to the rear destination box, when viewed from the back. The canal had been completed in 1799 and the local wharf was located to the left of the man in the gabardine mackintosh. The wharf was next to a large exploitable deposit of sand and gravel, and this was transported by barge around the West Midlands. Notable on the lamp posts in Yardley Road are the 'Ring Road' signs. (Birmingham Central Library)

Waiting to move off from the zebra crossing at the Swan in Yardley Road on 24 June 1963 is 2423 (JOJ 423), an exposed-radiator Crossley DD42/7 fitted with an attractive Crossley fifty-four seat body. Birmingham City Transport was criticised for its uninformative destination displays and 'Outer Circle 11' does at least seem at first sight to fall into this category. The bus shelters usually had some indication as to which suburb the bus was going next, and consequently the bus needed the minimum of information. Who said that Brummies lacked 'the old grey matter' – it was the strangers to the city who couldn't read! 2423 has just left the magnificent bus shelter to the right of the following Bedford TK lorry. The people who have just got off the No.11 bus are walking to the Yardley terminus of the No.58 route. On close inspection, the sign on the right, which survived into the 1970s, actually states: 'No entry. Trolley buses only', but the word 'trolley' was painted over after 1 June 1951 when the highly-efficient Coventry Road trolleybus service was abandoned. (W. Ryan)

The second, and perhaps best known, Swan public house, built in a Victorian, mock-Tudor style, dominated the Coventry Road junction from 1899 until it was unnecessarily pulled down in 1964, when the Swan underpass was constructed. The gable-ended building, again with false half-timbering, is the block of four shops in Yardley Road, which in this June 1935 scene had Lees's confectioners advertising itself as 'Our Sweet Shop'. The bus standing at the bus shelter opposite those shops – with Perry Barr on the blind – is one of the forty-seven Metro-Cammell-bodied Morris-Commercial Imperials, which dated from 1933. The lady pushing the antiquated pram across Church Road looks anxiously at the speeding Austin Sixteen Six, which has obscured the identification of the Imperial. About to overtake the bus is a Morris Minor Tourer, while further away, in Yardley Road, is one of the comparatively old-fashioned A.D.C. 507s of 1928 from the 296-337 class. On the right, is a six-wheeled Leyland TTBD2 trolleybus, waiting at the Yardley trolleybus station. Behind it is the former C.B.T. tram depot, which was closed in 1912 after being taken over by the Corporation. The building later became the premises of R.H. Collier & Co. who were car retailers; they became well-known in the Depression period for purchasing the stock of motor manufacturers who had gone bankrupt and then building up new cars from the existing stock of purchased parts. Colliers also seemed to acquire the sales franchises for some of the more obscure manufacturers. The large gable-end sign shows that in 1935, they were agents for Willys Overland, Manchester light commercial vehicles, Calcott, Clyno, Swift and Vulcan Cars, all of whom were victims of the slump between 1929 and 1933 and had ceased trading. Colliers themselves vacated the old tram depot premises in around 1964. (Birmingham Central Library)

Waiting to come out of Church Road and cross the Coventry Road junction opposite the Swan Hotel on 13 June 1934 is another outside staircase double-decker. This is another unusual vehicle because although 198 (OP 227) is a standard AEC 504 with a normal-looking Birmingham-style body, this was built by a Lincolnshire coachbuilder called Thompson who hailed from Louth. It is thought that these ten bodies for Birmingham were the only ones of this type built by Thompson, whose factory entrance was not tall enough to extract the completed buses. On the right is the site previously occupied by an old farmhouse, which had latterly been used by William Painter. He was the local Yardley undertaker, who thrived after the opening of Yardley cemetery in 1900. The eighteenth-century former farm buildings had recently been cleared in preparation for the building of a short-lived set of three-storey shops and flats. These were in turn replaced by the multi-storey Tivoli centre after the construction of the Swan underpass in 1967. Behind this empty site is the large Hardings Royal Steam Bakery. To the left are the 1890s buildings on the corner of Coventry Road and Church Road, which include a post office and a chemist's shop with one of those wonderful weighing machines with a ceramic body, almost hidden in the dark shadows beneath the sun awning. (Birmingham Central Library)

The new Swan Hotel, photographed in around 1966, soon after it had replaced its mock Tudor predecessor. The one fact most locals knew about the Sixties building was that it was the largest pub in the country. It has in turn been demolished, but not on this occasion replaced by another inn. (Birmingham Central Library)

four

South Yardley to Six Ways Erdington

Above: A 1926 AEC 504 with a Thompson H26/26RO body passes the Yardley Junior and Infant School on its way from the Yew Tree to the Swan in 1931, not long after the section of dual carriageway was opened. The school occupies the corner site where Church Road and Harvey Road meet. It was built in the Edwardian period and had typical school board tall-gabled windows so beloved of educationalist architects of the day. The turn into the left-hand section at the start of the new dual carriageway (near to the entrance to the Oaklands playing fields) was sufficiently sharp as to warrant the sign, already hidden by foliage, which warns: 'Keep to left carriageway'. (Birmingham Central Library)

Above: Standing outside the shops near the corner of Hob Moor Road at the now demolished Yew Tree public house is 1635 (GOE 635). It is on a No.11 route short-working to Bromford Lane and Tyburn Road. The bus is one of the awkwardly-styled Park Royal-bodied AEC Regent III RT types. The driver is giving a handsignal as he begins to pull away from the Yew Tree's scaffold-type bus shelter in the summer of 1959, as he continues to the turn-back point at the Fox and Goose. These buses could only be driven by Acocks Green's crew as they were the only bus drivers on the system to have been 'passed out' on them. With their powerful 9.6 litre AEC engines, air-controlled pre-selector gearboxes and a penchant for having an extremely problematic footbrake, to see them on any part of the Circle was a rare treat. (D. Richmond)

Opposite below: The local press in September 1930 were bombarded with letters by irate Outer Circle passengers complaining that they were not getting the 'new' buses which were operating on the No.34 and No.1A routes. They said that they had to make do with old-fashioned buses, which lacked comfortable seats and decent ventilation, and had solid tyres. In the end, they had to put up with the outside staircase buses for another six years, though they were fitted with pneumatic tyres and re-upholstered in an attempt to ensure that the undertaking got a full working life out of them. In 1931, a four-year-old A.D.C. 507 bus, 260 (OX 1536), with a locally-built Buckingham H26/26RO body, speeds along Church Road, South Yardley towards the almost new shops which were built around the Yew Tree. Parked outside the ladies' outfitters is a Ford Model A Fordor saloon, which was one of the last cars to be built at Ford's Trafford Park factory, outside Manchester, before it moved to the huge Dagenham plant at the end of 1931. The section of Church Road from Harvey Road and the Red Hill and Oaklands Recreation Ground on the other side of the road, down to the Yew Tree junction at Hob Moor Road, had been made into a dual carriageway around a year earlier. The intention was to widen the road from the Swan, but seventy-three years later it has yet to be done. (Birmingham Central Library)

Above: Station Road – between the Yew Tree and Stechford shopping centre – was lined with mainly Edwardian houses, varying in size between the large villa and attractive small terraces. Until the late 1950s, there was very little urban development to the north-east of Bordesley Green East, but early in the next decade two buildings were constructed that were a little out of place in terms of their size and style. On the vacant land alongside Bordesley Green East was the new police staion, while on the next corner nearer to Yardley Fields Road, and taking over part of the local recreation park, were the impressively modern Stechford swimming baths. They were built in 1961 and still remain a hugely popular local attraction. A Guy Arab IV of October 1954 vintage, 3088 (MOF 88), still looking like a Birmingham City Transport vehicle, but in fact owned by West Midlands PTE and painted in their lighter, mid-blue livery, passes the baths on its way to South Yardley on 21 October 1974. (C.C. Thornburn)

Opposite above: Yew Tree garage next to the Co-op on Stoney Lane on 31 August 1960. At this date, and for several years afterwards, the proprietor of the garage was David Geddie. The garage was built in around 1932 and is a handsome example of a pre-war garage, so different from the modern service station. (Birmingham Central Library)

Opposite below: Blakesley Hall, one of the main tourist landmarks on (or, more accurately, just off) the Outer Circle route, on a sunny autumn day in 2002. Of course, if photography had been invented in the sixteenth century, the view would have looked much the same, as this splendid Elizabethan yeoman's house has been on this site since 1590. It is one of the few remaining examples of a timber-framed farmhouse in the city. Built for Tudor yeoman Richard Smalbroke, the house is now owned by the city and is open free of charge to visitors in the summer months. (A. Spettigue)

A fine set of shop frontages along Station Road, September 1953. Among the shops leading from Lyttleton Road were Gazard's electrical repairs, the Ideal Benefit Society, Biddles confectioners at number 201 and the tobacconist Harvey's. (Birmingham Central Library)

Above: These shops are across the road from those in the previous photograph and are pictured around forty years earlier. It was a much more leisurely age before the Outer Circle came along and the shops were a typical mix of ironmongers, grocers and tobacconists. (Birmingham Central Library)

Left: An advertisement for Parkinson's stoves which were made at the company's factory in Station Road. One of Birmingham's best-known businesses, Parkinson's first manufactured gas cookers at premises in Bell Barn Road. The company subsequently expanded and moved to Sour Street, Spring Hill, before, in 1913, acquiring the eight-acre Stechford site. A report in the trade paper (the *Gas World*) in 1931 listed the trade names inseparably linked with the Stechford works. They included the New Suburbia cookers, the Ajusto oven heater regulator, the Treasure series of geysers, the Stechford gas-fire range and the Sunray gas-fire radiant. (Birmingham Central Library)

Stechford Station is situated 3½ miles east of Birmingham, which is about the average distance that the No.11 bus route is from the city centre. The first Stechford Station was opened as part of the London & Birmingham Railway as early as October 1844, when it was known as Stechford Gates. The station was only used for 'short' trains, which were local trains on the line between the newly-opened Curzon Street Station in Birmingham and Rugby, though it would be another two months before booking huts and platforms were built. In February 1882, a second station was constructed to the west of the original station, and the original level crossing in Station Road, known as Yardley Gates, was replaced by the overbridge, station buildings and booking hall. The two island platforms were reached from the booking hall on Station Road Bridge by way of a pair of covered flight of steps. The station came into its own in 1882, as an important joining-up point for trains, after the L & NWR opened its Grand Junction diversion line which travelled around Birmingham and on to the Stour Valley line at Handsworth. Unfortunately, it was this junction which caused a severe accident within sight of the station's road bridge. On 28 February 1967, an engineer's ballast train was returning to Coventry and had reached the points network to the west of the station. Because of the length of the train, it was decided to do some unauthorised manoeuvres at the exit from the Grand Junction line. At the crucial moment, this left the Diesel-Electric Bo-Bo Type 2 locomotive, D5002, overhanging the mainline between Birmingham and Coventry by a few inches. A four-car Electrical Multiple Unit, (E.M.U.) passenger hit the locomotive, killing the driver and eight passengers, with another sixteen being injured. (R.S. Carpenter)

The original Bull's Head was an early Victorian building which was built on the corner of Stechford Road and the old lane which was later to become Flaxley Road. This building, which featured the mounted head of a bull (with an evil look on its face, looking as if it had just charged through the upstairs wall) survived as a hostelry until the 1920s. This almost rural scene of June 1903 shows a little boy wearing a cap, beyond the fence, sitting on the grass bank in front of the then quite new houses

which were beginning to invade the water meadows of the River Cole. The shops on the right date from just before the turn of the twentieth century, and have a touch of the Arts and Crafts movement about them. The two carts are owned by Hardings the baker's, who survived until the 1970s and a baker's and confectioner's called Waldron, who, although selling Hovis bread, belongs to a long list of bakers who have long since gone out of business. (University of Birmingham)

The Bull's Head in Stechford Road stands on the south side of Stechford Bridge which crosses the River Cole. For many years, the land between the public house and the river was used by travelling fairgrounds as their winter quarters. It was a huge pub with elements of half-timbered Tudor mixed in somewhat curiously with mullion-windowed Jacobean wings dating from the turn of the twentieth century. It was originally an Ansells House, as it was when 259 (OX 1525), travelling towards Yardley, stood fully laden outside the pub on a sunny summer's day in 1934. This double-decker was a 1927 vintage A.D.C. 507 with an outside staircase and Short H26/26RO body, which would be scrapped the following year. (J. Cull)

By the mid-1960s, the Bull's Head was an Atkinson's-owned pub, which was strange as they had been taken over in 1959 by Mitchells & Butlers. The public house occupied a very large site with entrances in Flaxley Road, which is behind the bus. In the 1970s, the No.11 bus route was diverted from going up the causeway and over the railway line at Stechford Station in Station Road. Instead it followed the No.14 service into Flaxley Road, before turning into Iron Lane and then on to the steep rise up to the railway bridge. The pub was renamed the Manor Tavern, but it was too large to be a success and closed down in 2000. The bus is 3123 (MOF 123), a Crossley-bodied Daimler CVG6, which entered service as part of the Erdington tram replacement fleet on 4 July 1953. (M. Fenton)

Immediately beyond the junction with Stechford Road, which was followed by the No.55 bus route to Shard End, 2028 (JOJ 28), a Daimler CVD6 with a Metro-Cammell body, waits to pick up passengers outside Millward Brothers' ironmonger's shop in Stechford Lane. The bus is one of Perry Barr's fleet of refined pre-selector gearbox buses. Their Daimler CD6 8.6 litre engines were extremely quiet, but they did tend to burn a little more oil and as a result most only managed about fourteen years' service. 2028, still with the old-style gold fleet numbers, was one of the last three of this once hundred-strong class to be withdrawn, in August 1966. (A. Yates)

Alongside the River Cole at Stechford Bridge were the winter headquarters of a fairground, which had a collection of old caravans, lorries and old buses. Redundant second-hand buses were a good investment for circus folk and showmen because they could be bought for under £50 and used as living quarters as well as a towing vehicle. Pre-war S.O.S. single-deckers, previously built and supplied by the Birmingham & Midland Motor Omnibus Company (better known as Midland Red) were a useful but cheap purchase, as their value to independent bus operators was minimal. In a yard which looks very similar to the one at Stechford, all the accoutrements of a showman's winter quarters are present, with a former Trent Motor Traction bus (CH 9910), an S.O.S. IM6 of 1931, with a Short B34F body converted into a caravan with curtains and even a bay window. (A.B. Cross)

Above: Stechford Lane had been re-aligned in 1932 when the tram terminus for the No.10 route was moved into the central reservation. Approaching this junction with Washwood Heath Road and opposite the Beaufort Cinema is 1325 (FON 325). This was a very rare beast, being one of six similar Leyland Titan TD7s with Leyland H30/26R bodies which were originally intended for the Western Scottish Motor Traction Company, but whose completion was 'frozen' by the Ministry of War Transport. 1325 was finally completed after the department unfroze those vehicles or part-completed buses for delivery – it was diverted to Birmingham and entered service on 24 February 1942. Always allocated to Perry Barr garage, it is pictured making its way back home. Although they were fine-looking buses, the TD7 models were not very popular with drivers as they had an inordinately long time lag between changing gear ratios due to their large flywheels. This made them somewhat unsuitable for much of their work in the city – even though a clutch stop was fitted to them, which hastened the speed of gear changes, but this did nothing for the driver's painful clutch foot and ankle! (A. Yates)

Opposite below: One of Acocks Green garage's Crossleys – 2342 (JOJ 342) – negotiates the island at the Fox and Goose on its way towards Stechford on 3 January 1967. This bus spent all its working life at the same garage and was to be withdrawn within the next two months on the last day of February. To the right of the bus is a black-painted Ford Popular 103G, while behind the Crossley is a Bedford HA van, based on the Vauxhall Viva two-door saloon. The shops in Coleshill Road dated from the early 1920s but had retained the traditional feel of a suburban shopping centre before the onslaught of the supermarket all but obliterated the traditional shop. The shop with the striped awning was a case in point – being one of the fifty-one strong chain of Pearks Dairies grocery and provision dealers. Parked on the pavement outside Miss Stone's grocery shop in Coleshill Road is a Jaguar Mark II, which sports GB plates at a time when continental motoring was still a little unusual. (A. Yates)

Above: On 4 June 1950, a well-laden bus, 1720 (HOV 720), a Brush-bodied Leyland Titan PD2/1, crosses the No.10 route tram terminus at the Beaufort Cinema as it travels from Stechford Lane into Bromford Lane when working on the No.11 route. Its passengers are already standing up as the bus heels over on its nearside springs when travelling around the traffic island. The bus is being followed by a Standard Vanguard Phase I, while turning in front of the Beaufort Cinema is a Wolseley 12/48 Series III. The magnificent Tudor-styled Beaufort opened on 4 August 1929 and had one of the finest suburban cinema organs in the country. It was a two-manual, eight-octave Compton, which was moved as early as 1937 to the Abbey Road studios in London. The cinema closed on 19 August 1978. (T.J. Edgington)

Above: The terminus of the No.10 tram route was at the Fox and Goose public house at the junction of Bromford Lane, Stechford Lane and Washwood Heath Road. On 10 August 1939, a piano-front AEC Regent travels along Bromford Lane towards the Beaufort Cinema when working on the No.11 route, while a tram stands next to the Bundy Clock at the loading railings. Car 796 was one of the fifty E.M.B. air-brake cars built in 1928 and was fitted from new with a bow collector instead of a trolley pole. The tram is in need of a repaint, as on the rocker panel the rewritten legal lettering still looks fresh in comparison with the rest of the vehicle since it was changed in November 1937. The width of Coleshill Road beyond this point with its wide, open grass verges suggests that the intention was to extend the tram route beyond Hodge Hill to the Clock garage at Newport Road. (A.D. Packer)

Opposite below: With just a few days of municipal operation left in Birmingham, on 22 September 1969, a Guy Arab III Special, 2607 (JOJ 607), with a 26ft-long Metro-Cammell H30/24R body, trundles down Bromford Lane in a line of traffic waiting to get around the traffic island. Hidden by the bus is the Midland Counties Dairy distribution depot, while alongside it are the premises of Bromford Wallpapers. Careful examination of the front of 2607 shows that it had been fitted with one of the hideous fibre-glass radiator grills which were made at Tyburn Road as replacements for the original long-slatted ones for the last few years of Birmingham City Transport. (A. Yates)

Above: Somehow, photographs of this period taken of the city's main road junctions always look as if they have been staged. The same white-coated policeman directs the traffic, there are always workmen repairing the lights and the very occasional pedestrian. Here we have a another fine touch, a solitary would-be passenger waits for the No.11 to take him towards Erdington. All this at the Fox and Goose junction on 15 March 1932. (Birmingham Central Library)

Above: An atmospheric view of Bromford Lane at night – a prime candidate for a 'You are never alone with a Strand' advert. In fact, the rather stagey setting was because the photograph was demonstrating the efficiency of the new 'Mecra' lighting system, which had been put into operation a month beforehand, in October 1934. The van is an Austin 7 (WD 7444). (Birmingham Central Library)

Above: The Birmingham & Derby Junction Railway opened its line through to Whitacre on 10 February 1842, while on 16 May in the same year, a station called Bromford Forge was opened briefly. Over fifty years later on the same site, a new station called Bromford Bridge was opened on 9 March 1896 to cater for the traffic produced by the Bromford Racecourse. It was only used on race days. This was taken into Birmingham in the boundary adjustments of 1931, and the final horse-racing meeting took place on 21 June 1965, with the station closing seven days later. Not long after the bridge which carried Bromford Lane over the railway line was completed on 8 September 1924, looking from the platform towards the city centre, a fitted goods train makes its way towards Lawley Street goods yard, near to the city centre. (Birmingham Central Library)

Opposite below: On Monday 29 March 1948, the crowds rush to leave the Bromford Bridge Racecourse. The people, nearly all men, form an orderly queue for the buses, marshalled by just a few inspectors, safe in the knowledge that there are sufficient Corporation buses to get them away from the racecourse in a matter of minutes. Some of the punters are ignoring the buses and are walking towards Bromford Bridge Railway Station, which is beyond the leading bus. This vehicle is 1230 (FOF 230), a 1939-registered Daimler COG5 with a Metro-Cammell body, which will follow Bromford Lane as far as Wheelwright Road before turning onto Tyburn Road and off towards its stated destination – 'City'. Immediately behind it is one of the few Brush-bodied wartime Daimler CWA6s, which were numbered 1471-1474. In the distance, there is another line of buses parked just beyond the Bromford Inn facing Ward End, on the corner of Bromford Road. (D.R. Harvey Collection)

Above: Bromford Lane/Wheelwright Road. On 18 April 1963, the large metal-clad factory in Bromford Lane dominates the corner of Wood Lane is that owned by Birlec, who were leading exponents in the gas and electrical heat treatment industry. The factory, which had been owned by the Aston Chain and Hook Company, is just beyond the bridge over the Birmingham & Fazeley Canal. The Standard Ensign on the left is turning into Wheelwright Road alongside the premises of the Bromford Tube Company, who made extruded seamless steel tubes. The Esso service station had been built in the early 1960s and parked outside it is a 1958 London-registered Standard Super 10. Opposite the garage is a line of shops – including a coffee room and a newsagent, which would both obviously serve the local furnacemen – but in the block for many years was a corset shop! The Outer Circle bus route took the line being followed by the Morris Minor 1000 and Volkswagen 1200 De Luxe cars as they make their way to the junction with Tyburn Road, which was the next main road to cross the No.11 service. (Birmingham Central Library)

Opposite above: Tram 670 – a Brush-bodied 40hp sixty-three seater bogie car of 1924 – pulls away from the impressive green-painted wooden tram shelters at the junction of Tyburn Road with Bromford Lane, which disappears behind the tram over the distant Birmingham & Fazeley Canal bridge. It was across this junction that the Outer Circle bus, after stopping at the Navigation public house, crossed Tyburn Road. Tyburn Road was built by the Birmingham Corporation and the Dunlop Rubber Company. Throughout the First World War, Dunlop had to transport its munitions workers from Gravelly Hill to Fort Dunlop by barge along the Birmingham & Fazeley Canal. The completion of Tyburn Road led to the opening of the No.63 route as far as Holly Lane on 13 May 1920, enabling the Dunlop workers to have a more comfortable, though potentially less interesting ride to work. The No.79 route, on which 670 is working, was an extension to Pype Hayes Park, which was opened on 20 February 1927. (D.R. Harvey)

Above: Looking up Bromford Lane towards the Old Green Man pub on the right at the beginning of May 1931. A mug of ale or a flagon of cider were the preferred tipples when the landlord of the hostelry first opened its doors, possibly as long ago as 1307. Certainly one of the oldest pubs in the country, the Old Green Man (or the Lad in the Lane – it keeps changing names) is still serving pints today. The rural aspect of Bromford Lane by the pub was altered in 1921 when the road was widened as part of the scheme to build the new outer ring road. The local papers reported the 'sacrifice of a fine line of stately old elms ... the beauty spot has not been sacrificed without a pang by the city engineering department, but an ever-increasing volume of traffic, multiplied latterly by the Fort Dunlop enterprise, has demanded a wider highway to Erdington. They are to be succeeded by saplings which will afford shade to the next generation'. (Birmingham Central Library)

Above: The conversion of Bromford Lane into a dual carriageway took place in the early 1930s, when the last of the outside staircase buses delivered to the Corporation were less than two years old. One of the last of the A.D.C. 507s, 315 (VP 1179), speeds down the hill on 8 September 1932, passing the Green Man public house on its left as it approaches Tyburn Road. In the distance is the awkward dog-leg where Kingsbury Road crosses the much narrower Wood End Road. The mid-1920s municipal houses that lined this section of Bromford Lane were part of the Pype Hayes and Tyburn Road expansion of the period, which, unusually, left the Tame Valley side of Tyburn Road lined with factories and this side (away from the flood plain) purely with housing. (Birmingham Central Library)

Above: In Wood End Road in around 1958, 1664 (HOV 664) – one of Yardley Wood garage's allocation of Brush-bodied Leyland Titan PD2/1s – is showing a short-working display travelling towards Erdington. There were 100 of these buses, which were split between Yardley Wood and Perry Barr garages. It has just passed Rollaston Road, which was nearly opposite the Jaffray Hospital, and is in the shadows of the trees which are located in the seventeen-acre Rookery Park that had opened in 1905. Travelling in the opposite direction to Erdington is 2600 (JOJ 600), a Guy Arab III Special with a new-look front and a Metro-Cammell body. (R.F. Mack)

Opposite below: Travelling out of Wood End Road on 9 July 1974, negotiating the rather awkward curve across Kingsbury Road into Bromford Lane, is a Daimler CVG6 with a Crossley H30/25R, which was, by this time, twenty-one years old. For many years, Kingsbury Road was the route taken by Midland Red buses to Walmley and Tamworth, as they could not pick up in competition with the No.79 tram route along Tyburn Road. The result was that Corporation trams and bus routes were crossed three times by Midland Red buses as they left the city without impinging their agreement with B.C.T. The bus is 3135 (MOF 135), which was owned by West Midlands PTE, although it was to be a few years into the future before any appreciable change to the No.11 route would take place. (C.C. Thornburn)

Rookery Park house, formerly the Council House for Erdington Urban District, was acquired by the Erdington Council in 1905 from Dr Paget Evans for the sum of £37,250 and the grounds converted into a public park. The house and gardens were taken over by Birmingham in 1911, and the park (and especially the gardens in front of the house) remain charming stopping points on the Outer Circle route. (Birmingham Central Library)

The Outer Circle would have had another landmark if these proposed gas works had gone ahead on the site of the old Glenthorne estate on the Kingsbury Road. This rural scene was captured by the famous Birmingham photographer Sir Benjamin Stone in September 1904. Protestations by Erdington residents of the 'not in my back yard' variety forced the abandonment of the proposal. The driver of the horse and trap was Fred Bass, later caretaker at Rookery House. The Birches Green estate now occupies the site. (Birmingham Central Library)

This view is from around 1916. The hospital, which had been opened by the Prince of Wales in 1885, was designed by the architect Yeoville Thomason, who was responsible for the impressive Council House in Victoria Square. It was demolished in 1995 to be replaced by housing. (Birmingham Central Library)

The horse and two-wheeled cart are possibly delivering milk to the young girl dressed in a smock dress at the bottom of Wood End Road near the junction with Trafalgar Road. In these days before the First World War, Wood End Road was developed out of Erdington only as far as Deakin Road – at the end of the next row of tunnel-back housing. (Commercial Postcard)

Above: The first of the last class of exposed radiator buses ever bought by B.C.T. was 2396 (JOJ 396). This elegant Crossley DD42/7 had a Crossley H30/24R body and was fitted with the improved and more powerful Crossley HOE7/5B 8.6 litre engine. Although not fitted with pre-selector gearboxes (à la Daimler or Guy buses), they did have synchromesh gearboxes which were much easier to use than those on the contemporary Leyland Titan PD2/1s. 2396 is in Wood End Road, approaching the junction at Six Ways, Erdington, in 1966 on a short-working to Perry Barr, prior to returning to its garage in Wellhead Lane. (D.R. Harvey)

Above: After the deregulation of bus services in October 1986, certain alterations were made to the Outer Circle bus route. In Erdington, outer ring buses, instead of going straight across Six Ways from Reservoir Road into Wood End Lane, were diverted to run along Sutton New Road as far as Summer Road – a matter of little more than 200 yards – before undertaking a U-turn to face the Six Ways island, enabling the buses to pick up passengers at a more convenient point whilst posing less of a congestion problem to other road users. 2997 (F997 UOE), a Mark II MCW Metrobus, turns at what is now called Central Square while working the No.11C route on 3 February 2001. (D.R. Harvey)

Opposite below: On 2 September 1951, one of Perry Barr garage's exposed-radiator Crossley DD42/7s stands at the junction of Wood End Road (in the foreground) and Gravelly Hill North (off the picture to the left). On this corner, the bus stopped for the Six Ways, Erdington passengers outside the local branch of the Birmingham Municipal Bank. Beyond the large tram shelters in the middle of Six Ways, a 637 class eight-wheel tram leaves the shelters and takes to the reserved track in Sutton New Road. This dual carriageway was opened on 25 September 1938 in order to take the No.2 tram route out of Erdington High Street. This alteration to the Erdington tram route was the last new route section to be built in Birmingham. The eighteen-month-old Crossley will cross Six Ways and turn into Reservoir Road between the tall gable-roof houses, which almost seem to guard the entrance to the road out to Stockland Green. (Unknown)

In a quest to gain experience of operating a 30ft long by 8ft wide bus, the second Crossley Bridgemaster to be built (a demonstrator MB3RA which appeared at the 1956 Commercial Motor Show) was purchased in August 1957. Registered 9 JML, the bus had an outdated specification, having a small AV470 engine, albeit turbo-charged, a manual four-speed synchromesh gearbox and an attractive, but open-platform, seventy-two seat Crossley body. It was compared with products from Daimler (and, slightly later, with Guy Motors and Leyland), so in view of its specification, it was something of a surprise that this bus was purchased at all. After it was purchased in August 1957, it was numbered 3228 and continued operating from Lea Hall garage almost exclusively on the No.14 service on which it had been initially demonstrated. The bus rarely made excursions onto the other services operated by Lea Hall, so to see 9 JML on even a short-working of the Outer Circle was indeed a rare event, even though it is only displaying the unhelpful 'service extra' destination blind. It is turning into Wood End Road from Six Ways, Erdington, where the 1960s shops had replaced the impressive Victorian Baptist Church and Sunday School on the corner with the High Street. (R.F. Mack)

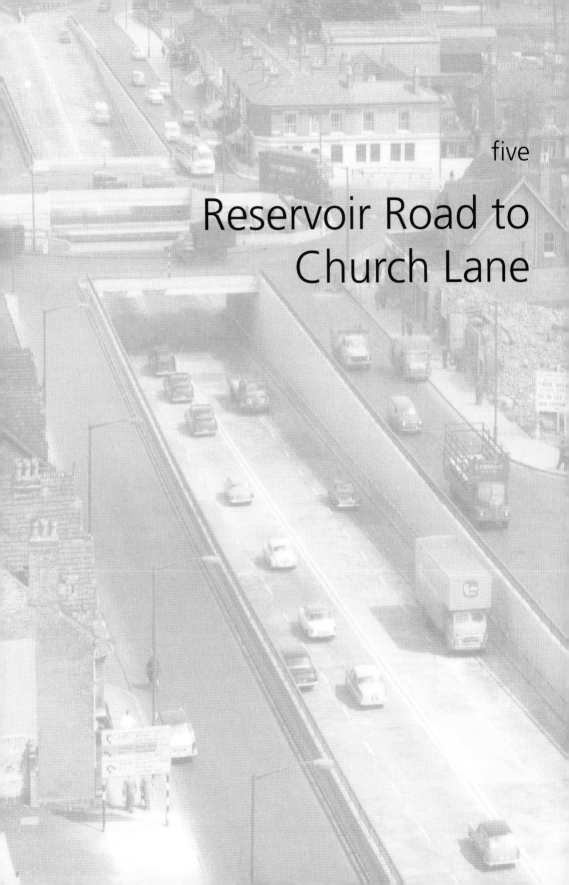

five

Reservoir Road to
Church Lane

Above: Standing at Stockland Green, with the early 1920s shops and houses behind him, the driver of 2973 (JOJ 973), a Metro-Cammell-bodied Guy Arab IV, opens the door to climb into his cab. It is the last day of May 1962 and the bus driver had only just 'pegged' the Bundy Clock. 2973, is obviously running late as not only is it already pretty full, but the next Outer Circle bus, 2520 (JOJ 520), a 1950-built Crossley-bodied Crossley DD42/7, is already in sight. The buses have just passed Highcroft Hospital and on the other side of the road, scarcely visible even from the top deck of a No.11, is Erdington Reservoir. At one time, the field above the reservoir was used as the home pitch for the City of Birmingham's Water Department football team. (A. Yates)

Opposite above: When the Outer Circle bus route was finally completed, the little single-deck Daimler CK2s were replaced by virtually new outside-staircase double-deckers. The last batch, numbered 296–337, were to be the backbone of the Outer Circle's bus service for the next six years or so, even when complaints were made in the local press about riding in uncomfortable, cold conditions. Standing outside the Fondella refreshment rooms is 297 (VP 1161), an A.D.C. 507 with a Short H24/26RO, which entered service on 16 November 1928 and was one of the last of the type to be withdrawn on 31 July 1937. A lady wearing a heavy coat is about to get on the bus, which will then depart for Erdington over the crest of the distant hill on Reservoir Road. On the left is the inner ring bus stop which stands on what had been, until about three years previously, a tiny triangle of bushes known as the Green. In the foreground are the tram tracks, which had been extended from the shopping centre in Stockland Green to Short Heath in June 1926. (N.C. Meachem)

Above: One of the first exposed-radiator Crossleys to be withdrawn was 2348 (JOJ 348), on 31 May 1964, after severe nearside accident damage. It is parked at the passenger bus stop and railings outside Millarde's ladies' outfitters – which stood between George Mason's grocery shop chain and Stockland Green Post Office – in happier (albeit rainier) days, in around 1951. This bus is parked in the same place as the one in the previous photograph. Behind the bus on the corner of Streetly Road and Marsh Hill is the Stockland Inn, which opened on 24 November 1924 and had been designed in a mock-Jacobean stone-fronted style by Mitchells & Butlers brewery. (A.M. Wright)

Above: On 16 July 1923, the No.11 route was extended from Erdington to Stockland Green, while on 12 November of the same year, the route was further extended to Perry Barr. It was at first operated by ten Daimler CK2s, nine of which, 81-88 (OL 1714-1721), were bodied by Strachan & Brown with twenty-four seats. This is the odd one out, with its slightly smaller Buckingham B21F body, and was numbered 80 (OK 9852). One of the nine is parked outside Fondella's confectionery shop and tea rooms. Behind the bus is Wilkins chemist shop, which was on the corner of Slade Road – the first in a terrace of shops which served Stockland Green. (N.C. Meachem)

Above: On leaving Stockland Green, the Outer Circle route descended the steep Marsh Hill. Partly hidden by the immature trees is the 1935-vintage 737 (AOP 737), a Metro-Cammell H26/22R-bodied Daimler COG5. Marsh Hill had been widened in 1923 when the houses on both sides of the hill were constructed, although the whole scheme had been planned before (but delayed by) the outbreak of the First World War. On the left behind the sign is Marsh Hill Junior and Infants School, while between the shops on the right and the approaching Outer Circle bus, is the Open Air School. This was built in a very airy, almost kindergarten-like style, for what were then called 'delicate' children. The main shop on the right was the Marsh Hill Post Office and behind it were some allotments on land belonging to Grove Farm. (N.C. Meachem)

Opposite below: In the summer of 1925, after the No.11 route had been extended beyond Perry Barr to the Kings Head, 82 (OL 1715), the second of the Strachan & Brown-bodied Daimler CK2s (which entered service on 18 October 1923), is at the top of Marsh Hill outside the newly opened Stockland Inn. It was during this penultimate extension that the No.11 route was given the name Outer Circle. The tram standing next to the Green at the Stockland Green terminus in Slade Road is one of the M.R.C.W.-bodied 637-661 class, which entered service towards the end of 1923. The No.1 tram route was extended from Stockland Green on 23 June 1926 as the No.78 route, just two and a half months after the No.11 service was completed (on 7 April). (D.R. Harvey Collection)

Above: The first post-war bus withdrawal occurred after this accident, which happened at the bottom of Marsh Hill. When descending the hill on an icy January morning in 1961, 1530 (GOE 530), a Daimler CVA6 with an M.C.C.W body, skidded and overturned onto its nearside. Most of the nearside body pillars were distorted – two or three years previously, this might have been repaired, but as these CVA6s were approaching their second recertification, it was decided (after nearly nine months of storage) not to repair the bus and it went to the 'Great Scrapyard in the Avon', owned by Birds of Stratford. (S. Calder)

Oppositve, above: At the bottom of Marsh Hill, in the distance behind the bus, this road turned quite sharply almost due south to become Brookvale Road. Here it ran parallel to an overflow channel between the Upper Witton Reservoir and the lake in Brookvale Park. The bus, 2568 (JOJ 568) – a 1950 short-length Guy Arab III – is standing opposite a short row of gabled council houses built in the Arts and Crafts style in Boulton Walk. These lie across a green on land bisected by the artificial stream. The gentleman standing behind the bus is crossing the road to where, slightly to his left, there is a row of shops which includes a Wrensons grocery shop and a municipal bank. The bus is facing Witton (which is due south) and is approaching the site of Witton Hall, which had been built in the early eighteenth century as the manor house for Witton. It was sold in 1907 as an old people's home and today the site is run as the Steward Centre. (A. Yates)

Above: Brookvale Park and Lake. The lake is actually an old reservoir constructed in the 1850s. It became redundant after the completion of the Welsh Water Scheme for the city and was purchased by Erdington Council in 1909, the water and the land around it being converted to an attractive park. The water area occupies about eighteen acres. On summer days youngsters paddle in the brook or play in the sand there and enjoy in imagination a seaside holiday in the fine bracing air of this upland valley. (Birmingham Central Library)

Above: The chapel at Witton Cemetery, June 1958. Witton was the first of the council cemeteries in the city, opening for burials in 1863. There were three different chapels in order to cater for Church of England, Roman Catholic and Nonconformist services. A separate Jewish cemetery on the site was acquired by the Jewish community in 1869. The management of the cemetery is a major operation, and the provision of effective security to cover the 103-acre site has been a serious concern to local residents and relatives of loved ones in recent times. (Birmingham Central Library)

Above: Brookvale Road salvage depot was opened on 9 April 1924 and occupied the site between Moor Lane, which skirted Witton Cemetery, and the BCN's Tame Valley Canal. By burning its own refuse, the plant produced sufficient steam to generate enough electricity for all the recharging needs of the Corporation's battery-powered fleet of dustcarts allocated to the depot. In this 1927 line-up of the Brookvale Road depot's nineteen-strong fleet, the highest level of the building towering above the vehicles is a ramped roadway with a 1 in 22 gradient, which the returning dustcarts had to climb before disgorging their salvage into the furnaces below. In this view, all the different manufacturers' battery-powered electric dustcarts are on parade. From the left, the first four are Ransomes Orwell 5 tonners (the first two being numbered 47 and 48), while the next three are respectively a rare 5 ton Electromobile (OM 4327), one of the prototype G.V. 5 tonners of 1923 (OL 4327), which had been manufactured in Tyseley, and a smaller 31/2 ton Garrett. These three look more like contemporary steam lorries than battery vehicles. The rest of the dustcarts are all bonneted 5-ton Garretts, built in 1925. The depot closed when the proposals for the elevated section of the M6 motorway were announced. It was replaced by a new salvage works in nearby Perry Barr in September 1971. (B.W. Ware)

Opposite below: There were numerous points on the Outer Circle route that were over-run by other bus services. Over the twenty-five-mile route, there were points in Harborne, Cotteridge, Acocks Green and Stechford which were shared with services going to and from the city centre. The length of Brookvale Road from Witton Square to the Ridgeway was shared with the cross-city No.5 and No.7 routes from as early as 26 September 1927, as the flag on the top of the bus stop shows. The bus has just left that stop, located on the corner of Moor Lane, while behind the wooden fence and bushes on the left is the Brookvale salvage depot. On 4 June 1937, trade looks a little dead for the masons, Roddis and Nourse, whose main trade was in the fifty-three-acre Witton Cemetery. The tall brick boundary wall is being passed by a Corporation bus – 535 (OC 535). This is an almost two-year-old Morris-Commercial Imperial with a Morris 7.7 litre petrol engine and a Metro-Cammell body which is working on the No.5 route to Perry Common. (Birmingham Central Library)

Above: A row of cottages on Brookvale Road, looking from the Tame Valley Canal Bridge towards Wyrley Road. This row of terraced houses was built around 1914, on what was then largely farmland. The fine original windows pictured here in October 1955 have now all been replaced. On the other side of the bridge is the Barn social club. (Birmingham Central Library)

Opposite above: One of Ansells Brewery's Austin A40 pick-up vans with a fitted top cover stands outside the mock-Tudor Yew Tree public house in Brookvale Road, on a typical wet August Sunday in 1956. In the distance, that apparently rare event of a bus being sighted on the No.11 route on a Sunday has just occurred. 2026 (JOJ 26) – a Daimler CVD6, a very quiet and refined vehicle – would be the type of bus not to offend any ears as it glided by. It is travelling towards the GEC factory complex, while to the right of the parked Hillman Minx Phase VIII are some iron railings. These marked 'the picturesque, tree-lined water meadows' of the River Tame, which realistically at this time was vying with the Tees, the Thames and the Lagan in Belfast to be Britain's most polluted river. (Birmingham Central Library)

Above: The GEC factory site at Witton, currently on offer for development and only used for match-day parking for the nearby Villa Park. This rather stark view is from February 1954, and was taken for the City's Engineering Department. (Birmingham Central Library)

GEO. KYNOCH, ESQ., M.P.
(President of the Aston Villa Football Club).

Left: The Scottish Victorian businessman George Kynoch, the founder of Kynochs, which was the country's largest ammunition company at one time. The original factory from which Kynochs developed was Pursall and Phillips, percussion cap makers, who were situated in the gun quarter in Whittall Street until 1859, when an explosion killed nineteen of the company's seventy employees. The firm then moved out to what was then a more rural area. In 1962, Kynochs was renamed IMI and earlier this year (2003), it was announced that IMI were leaving the site which was being sold to the Prudential. The present site covers about ninety-five acres but at its height it dominated this part of Witton, occupying twice that amount of land. (Birmingham Central Library)

Opposite above: Brookvale Road was used by both the Outer Circle and the No.7 Portland Road bus services, which was very useful during the rush hour for the nearby GEC factory. This company produced dynamos, electrical plant and switchgear on this site, as well as traction motors – many of which were supplied to Birmingham for their trams and all their Leyland trolleybuses. Bus 393 (OG 393), an AEC Regent 661 fitted with an English Electric piano-front styled body, travels over the River Tame bridge which separates Brookvale Road and the distant mock half-timbering of the Yew Tree public house and Witton Road in the foreground. The bus had been involved in experiments using creosote as a fuel in March 1933, and during the war would be one of only four buses in the class to be painted in an all-over grey livery. Four cyclists travel away from Witton, possibly from the nearby Kynocks factory, and are following an almost new Austin Cambridge. Visible to the left of the bus and alongside the GEC factory are the Hardy Spicer Works, which manufactured needle bearings, universal joints and propeller shafts for the motor industry. (Birmingham Central Library)

Opposite below: Witton Station Bridge and the entrance to the IMI factory in 2002. The station opened in 1876, enabling Astonians to take the train directly to Aston. The bridge is painted in claret and blue in recognition of the fact that Villa Park is just round the corner. (A. Spettigue)

Above: Witton tram depot is located in Witton Lane, barely 100 yards from Witton Square and the Outer Circle bus route. It also lies in the shadow of the 'Temple of Dreams' – Villa Park! Here, two open-balcony four-wheelers (320 and 372), the totally-enclosed 342 (nicknamed the 'armoured car'), and the Brush-built bogie car 606 stand in the four entrance doors on 23 March 1950. Witton depot had been opened by the Birmingham & Aston Tramways in 1882 for steam trams, which were taken over on behalf of Aston U.D.C. by C.B.T. when the original lease expired. Just over a year later, on 6 October 1904, it was converted to electric tram operation, with a capacity for thirty-eight trams on seven roads. Witton tram depot was used by the Corporation from 1 January 1912 and led a fairly uneventful life until 4 December 1940 when it had a direct hit from a bomb, which caused the roof to collapse onto the trams inside. Fifteen tramcars were so badly damaged that they were subsequently broken up. The depot was re-roofed at the end of the war and was finally closed on 1 October 1950, though for the next three years it was used for scrapping no less than 247 tramcars. While Miller Street, the last surviving operating depot, was being converted to buses prior to the final tramway abandonment, up to thirty trams were stabled each night at Witton, with the crews having to 'book on' first at Miller Street. It was then used to store buses until about 1955 when it was sold to Dents (and later Thomas Startin) as a car showroom. After they closed, the building fell into disrepair but could not be demolished because of the stone inscription above the trams which reads 'Borough Of Aston Manor Tramways Depot'. It was reopened in 1988 as the Aston Manor Transport Museum, where many interesting old relics are to be found amongst the well-restored buses. (A.N.H. Glover)

Opposite below: The cover of the Aston Villa programme for 17 April 1926, the first home game for which supporters could arrive on the Outer Circle. Spurs were the opposition and the Villa won by three goals to nil. The programme notes were spent denying press rumours that the club were about to sell their star forward, Billy Walker. Walker missed the Spurs game, along with team-mates Tom Mort and Dicky York, because all three were playing for England against the 'Auld Enemy' Scotland at Old Trafford that Saturday. There was no postponement for international matches in those days. Despite the presence of the three Villa players, however, England went down by a single goal to Scotland, continuing a dismal run of five defeats out of six. How times have changed! (Birmingham Central Library)

Above: With the Kynochs Works towering over Witton Square, the mad dash for the waiting Villa Park football specials at the end of a game is well underway in this 1935 scene. Three of the buses, including those parked outside the Co-operative shop, are outside staircase A.D.C. 507s, while on the extreme right is 494 (OV 4494) – a 1931 AEC Regent 661, with a Metro-Cammell metal-framed, piano-front style body. The bus going to Harborne, however, is the most interesting one. It is the unique M.C.C.W.-bodied Guy Arab, 208 (OC 8208), which was fitted from new with a Gardner 6LW 8.4 litre diesel engine. Looking at first glance like one of the Morris-Commercial Imperials, it had a longer bonnet and a distinctively wide radiator. What is surprising is that no more were purchased, as after 1934 the Daimler COG5 with the smaller 5LW Gardner engine reigned supreme in the city's bus fleet. (D.R. Harvey)

Above: Aston Lane, looking up Wellhead Lane in July 1939. A sweetshop and tobacconist's, Newbery's is the corner shop on the site now occupied by the plastic factory, Tufnols, whose emissions regularly waft across the campus of the University of Central England, situated just behind the factory. George Ellison still remains on the other side of Wellhead Lane. (Birmingham Central Library)

Opposite above: There is something odd about the car that has turned into Aston Lane from Birchfield Road, Perry Barr, on 15 September 1960. The problem is that it is a Hillman Minx Phase VI, which was manufactured by the Rootes Group during 1953, yet it has an OJW-registration, which was first licensed in Wolverhampton in March 1955. Something's wrong here! On the corner of Aston Lane, just round the corner from the Crown and Cushion public house, is the Perry Barr branch of Barclays Bank, with its concrete Portland-effect ground floor. Beyond the 'Not in use' bus stop is the Perry Barr Methodist Church, with its large south-facing rose window. All the buildings on the right were demolished as part of the Perry Barr underpass scheme, and this end of Aston Lane was made into a short length of dual carriageway. Temporary replacement shops were built and these lasted for nigh on forty years! In the distance, behind a Bedford lorry, is a No.11 bus at the Wellhead Lane-Stoneleigh Road junction. The bus is one of the nearby Perry Barr garage's allocation from the 1656–1755 class of Leyland Titan PD2/1s with Brush H30/24R bodywork. (Commercial Postcard)

Above: This may look like a photograph of a typical old-fashioned library, but the reason why this view of Birchfield Library appeared in the local press in January 1953 was because the building had just been modernised and reorganised. The photograph shows the librarian, Miss A. Kauer, helping a borrower choose a book. This had been the system for the previous seventy years, but an extension to the library and an infusion of an extra 3,000 books meant that borrowers would, for the first time, be able to wander among the shelves and choose their own reading. Miss Kauert told the *Evening Mail*: 'Many people will be glad to have a complete freedom of choice but things won't be the same'. (Birmingham Central Library)

The problem in Perry Barr was the lack of imagination in naming the public houses. The Old Crown and Cushion, which had stood on the corner of Wellington Road, was replaced with this large pre-war building, making it the 'new' Old Crown and Cushion. In the early 1930s, on the opposite side of Birchfield Road, there was a beer retailer called Frank Deakin, whose Ansells-owned premises was called the New Crown and Cushion, which was now older than the Old Crown and Cushion! Confused? The Outer Circle bus crosses Birchfield Road from Witton Lane into Wellington Road, where the vehicles at the traffic lights include a Ford 300E 5 cwt van, followed by a Hillman Minx and a Ford Thames 16 cwt van. Parked on the forecourt of the public house on 25 February 1959 is a 1938 Morris Ten Series II, a Hillman Husky and on the site of the old walled beer garden is an early post-war Morris 10 Series M. (Birmingham Central Reference Library)

Perry Barr was the terminus of the No.6 tram route, which stopped just short of the railway bridge that also led down to Perry Barr Station. The row of shops on the left included Wilkins' chemist shop, with its sign for 'Iron Jelloids', and the New Crown and Cushion (with the large lantern outside it), which was part of the row of Victorian shops. Beyond that is the blurred shape of an outside staircase double-decker bus entering Aston Lane on its way to Witton and Erdington on the Outer Circle bus route, dating the picture to around 1928. The tram is car 11 which was on its way into the city. This was one of the original 1 - 20 class of open-top E.R. & T.C.W. bogie cars, which opened the first Corporation tram route from Steelhouse Lane to Aston Brook Street on 4 January 1904. In July 1907, car 11 received a top cover, but it was completely destroyed on the night of 9 April 1941 when Miller Street was hit by an oil bomb, becoming one of twenty-four to be demolished in that night's air-raid. On the corner of Wellington Road is the original Old Crown and Cushion building, which dated from around the 1860s. The pub was opposite Aston Villa's Wellington Road ground, and its claim to fame was its use as the headquarters of the infant Aston Villa FC, from 1876 until they moved into their new ground, Villa Park, on 17 April 1897. This was just one week after they had won the FA Cup against Everton in their double-winning year. A glass-roofed urinal was let into the wall of the beer gardens between the pub and the pollarded trees. The trees were felled in the 1930s, but the open space proved useful a few years later when the Old Crown and Cushion was replaced with a huge road-house style building. (Commercial Postcard)

Above: The demolition gangs are all but finished on the site of the Birchfield Cinema, which had stood on the corner of Birchfield Road and Bragg Road. The Perry Barr underpass was opened in 1962 and was one of several underpasses to be built in Birmingham at this time. On 31 May 1962, the underpass is virtually new, its modern look contrasting with the vehicles using it, which look as though they belong to another era. In the background is Witton Lane with the Methodist Church, while on the left is the Old Crown and Cushion public house, which has lost most of its front car park with the building of the underpass. Negotiating the traffic island in front of Barclays Bank is an almost-new Midland Red D9. The bus leaving the bus shelter outside Wrensons is 3138 (MOF 138), a Daimler CVG6 with a Crossley body, which is travelling into Birmingham on the No.52 service from the Beeches Estate. (Birmingham Central Library)

Opposite above: Wellington Road, at the junction with Grosvenor Road, in February 1955. The motorcar dealer was Grays, a well-remembered local landmark from the Thirties but since pulled down to be replaced by housing. Behind Grays in Grosvenor Road was John Drew & Sons, millers. The mill is commemorated in the name Old Mill Close for the new development on the mill site. (Birmingham Central Library)

Opposite below: The Calthorpe Arms, on the corner of Wellington Road and Wood Lane, in 1960. Along with the Grove pub (further along the route towards Handsworth Wood), this provides an attractive refuelling stop on this part of the route. The Calthorpe Arms has recently been repainted and still looks rather splendid with its attractive gas light. However, the decision to pull down the houses on the far left of the pub to create a beer garden and car park is not to everyone's taste. (Andrew Maxam)

So, trolleybuses *did* get onto the Outer Circle? Well, yes and no! When the Coventry Road trolleybuses were abandoned on the night of Saturday 30 June 1951, all seventy-four were sold to W.T. Bird of Stratford-upon-Avon. Their contract was to clear Arthur Street depot after the closure of the Lode Lane service on the Friday evening and complete the task by Sunday evening. As all the trolleybuses had to be transported to Stratford behind an ex-RAF lorry, it was quickly realised that they would not be able to fulfil their aim. As a result, eight six-wheelers and one each of the COX and FOK-registered Leyland four-wheelers were taken to Cunliffe's yard in Wellington Road near to the railway bridge, where they remained until Birds collected them in the spring of 1952. The only Leyland TB5 was trolleybus 73, which could be identified by the guttering around the upper-saloon corner pillars. (D.R. Harvey Collection)

Cottages in Church Lane in 1933, in a photograph taken by Hilda Jeffries. This part of the route is an exception to the general observation that the best housing is to be found on the south side of the city, as this part of Handsworth Wood boasts a considerable number of stylish properties set against tree-lined roads. (Birmingham Central Library)

St Andrews Church, which was consecrated on 30 January 1909. This splendid church was the last created out of the Handsworth parish, as the district expanded very rapidly in the nineteenth century. The inscription on the foundation stone records that it was laid by the Earl of Dartmouth on 19 October 1907. The architect was William Henry Bidlake. Immediately behind the church in Slack Lane lies a hidden jewel – the old listed cottages in Slack Lane, which used to be Handsworth Town Hall – along with the church, these are more than worth a stop off the No.11 at this point. There is an excellent history of the church on its website which can be found at www.standrews-handsworth.org.uk. (Birmingham Central Library)

The lightest of the three lightweight double-deckers, 3002 (LOG 302), stands at the Handsworth Wood Bundy Clock in Church Lane outside the 1960s luxury blocks of flats which extend around the corner into Handsworth Wood Road. The bus is just short of the junction with Wellington Road, Hamstead Road and the nearby Parish Church of St Mary. Although the tower is part twelfth and part fifteenth century, most of the rest of the church dates from its 1820 reconstruction. It is also the final resting place of Matthew Boulton, James Watt and William Murdock. Unusually, it is the conductor who is 'pegging the clock', rather than the driver. 3002 was one of a handful of Daimler CL5Gs to be constructed in the quest to improve fuel consumption. It has a fifty-five-seater Metro-Cammell body, which was a curious mixture of that manufacturer's Orion body and standard B.C.T. trim. The whole imbalance was completed by it being the only short-length half-cab bus to have a sliding door and an extremely square rear dome. This bus is now preserved in the Aston Manor Transport Museum. (J.C. Walker)

The No.26 tram service to Oxhill Road was opened on 20 November 1912 and terminated at the junction of Stockwell Road on the left and Rookery Road on the right. The Outer Circle bus route followed the tram route from Grove Lane before turning into Rookery Road and moving on to Soho Road. Brush-built bogie tramcar 601, seen in pristine condition here in 1938, was built in the late spring of 1920, but would soon be transferred to Selly Oak for most of the rest of its operating life. Opposite the tram, located on a traction pole, is a diamond-shaped ring road sign, while on the nearest lamp-post is a newly installed litter bin. Walking into the middle of Oxhill Road would have been quite difficult despite the lack of traffic, but it is perhaps a little surprising that the still quite new Belisha crossing was located at the end of Rookery Road where the four young men are standing. (W.A. Camwell)

By September 1980, over forty years later, the trees have grown along with the amount of traffic, and the Belisha beacons have been replaced by panda crossings. The trams have long since gone, yet little else has changed on the corner of Oxhill Road and Rookery Road – even the late nineteenth-century shops look more prosperous. On the right in Rookery Road, working on the No.11C service, is 7004 (WDA 4T) – one of five Leyland Titan TNLXBs with Park Royal H47/26F bodywork – which had entered service in January 1979. (Birmingham Central Library)

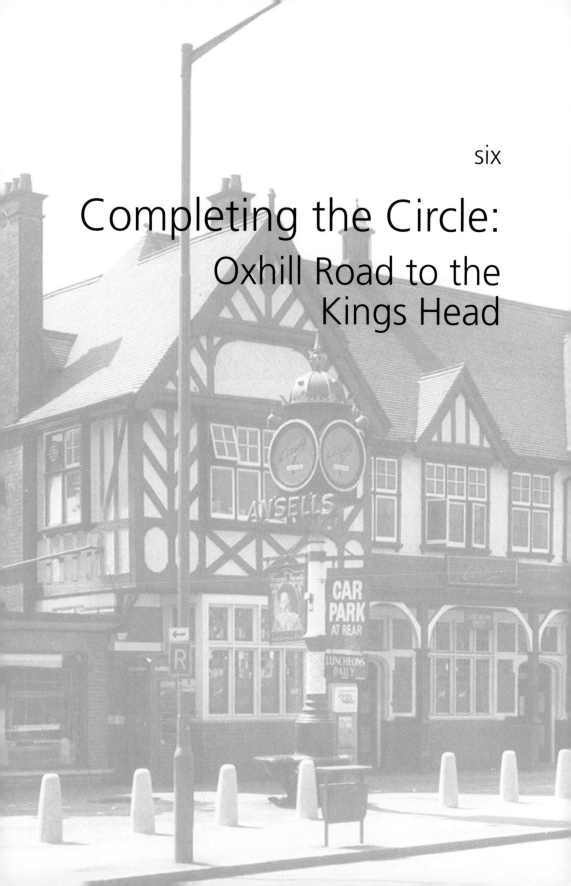

six

Completing the Circle:
Oxhill Road to the Kings Head

Above: At the western end of Rookery Road, the No.11 bus route reached Soho Road, which is to the immediate right of the tramcar. Car 629, a Brush-bodied bogie tram built in 1921, is travelling into the city on the No.28 route, which was a short-working of the main line Dudley (74) and Wednesbury (75) routes to the New Inns. this was the terminus of the C.B.T. cable trams which operated from Colmore Row between 1888 and 1911. The tram is standing at the northern end of the extensive Handsworth shopping centre and is opposite the Mitchells & Butlers-owned Queens Head public house. The motorcar in the foreground, parked on the wrong side of the road, is a 1934 Standard Ten. (Commercial Postcard)

Above: Looking down Soho Road from the junction with Queens Head Road in around 1966. The shop on the right-hand corner, Withers the newsagent's, is now an estate agency. Opposite the first lamp-post on the left is Cannon Street Memorial Baptist Church. This was opened in 1930 at a cost of £7,000. The name commemorated the mother church of the Birmingham Baptists, which itself had been founded in 1737 and closed in 1879. Perhaps the most colourful and heart-warming scene to be found on the Outer Circle route nowadays is on Sunday mornings, when the predominantly black congregation spills out onto the pavement in front of the church in a dazzling array of 'Sunday best' clothes. (Birmingham Central Library)

Opposite above: Situated on the corner of the main Rookery Road and Farnham Road is the large Trinity Methodist Church. This red-brick Gothic church, with its heavy buttresses, rather dwarfs many of the surrounding contemporary late nineteenth-century shops and houses. In the next road (off the picture to the left) is Uplands Road, and it was here that some of the last German air-raid damage to be inflicted on Birmingham happened on 13 August 1942. Rookery Road is followed for all of its length from Oxhill Road to Soho Road by the Outer Circle route, and here, in September 2002, a Mk II MCW Metrobus – 2456 (NOA 456X) – passes the Methodist Church on its way towards Soho Road, passing the Farcroft Hotel on the corner of Albion Road. This was built in the early 1920s in an expansive mock-Tudor, half-timbered style. There was a plan to extend the No.26 tram route from Oxhill Road along Rookery Road and into Soho Road, thereby making a large loop to serve this part of Handsworth, but the scheme never came to fruition. (A. Spettigue)

Above: The original Red Lion Inn on Soho Road was a coaching inn which had developed over the years since the days of Henry VIII. In the Civil War, the pub's stables were used by Cromwell's Model Army during the skirmishes around Birmingham in the early part of April 1643. The frontage of the old Red Lion stood in front of a courtyard, which in 1870 had played a part in the early horse-bus operations by the Birmingham Omnibus Company. In the foreground, in around 1895, amongst the mud and the stone setts, are the C.B.T. cable tram tracks which served Handsworth for twenty-three years. The present pub was built on the same site in 1902 by the Holt Brewery. (Birmingham Central Library)

Opposite above: The fact that it was celebrating its centenary seems to have been lost on the owners of the magnificent, but neglected, Red Lion public house in Soho Road. The Red Lion has suffered from planning blight, as the proposed ring road was planned to continue across Soho Road from Boulton Road. This scheme seems to have been shelved and it is to be hoped that a refurbishment can quickly take place. The building was designed by James and Lister Lea for the Holt Brewery. It was flattered with plum-coloured terracotta on the ground floor with buff above that. The building has heraldic lions, Flemish tracery and Jacobean tracery, as well as pediments at practically every horizontal level. The gap between the pub and the multi-gabled shops used to be the premises of a second-hand car lot, but this disappeared in the 1990s. The sign posts point to the next section of the Outer Circle bus route and the outer ring road, which is now numbered as the A4040. (A. Spettigue)

Above: One of the last of the former Birmingham City Transport Crossley-bodied Daimler CVG6s back-loaders in service – 3134 (MOF 134) – swings left out of Boulton Road in around 1976. It is travelling on a No.11E short-working to Perry Barr and back to its home garage. 3134 has managed to take up half of the opposite carriageway as it is hauled around into Soho Road, hiding the six tall-gabled shops that stand next to the Red Lion pub. These buses, along with the similar-looking Guy Arab IVs, were already past their normal life expectancy by the early 1970s, but would have to soldier on working the Outer Circle, which was the last conductor-manned route in the city, until 31 October 1977. (D.R. Harvey)

Above: Boulton Road was named after the pioneer industrialist Matthew Boulton, who had set up his pioneering Soho Manufactory in 1762. This initially used the water power from the nearby Hockley Brook, and within twenty years was using James Watt's successful steam beam engine. Behind the bus is Soho Road and its row of shops with the gable attic ends, which stood next to the Red Lion public house. To the right is the Cross Guns public house, which dates from the 1920s, occupying the corner with Barn Lane. 2981 (E981 VUK) – an MCW Metrobus Mk II with a Metro-Cammell H43/30F body – has just turned from Soho Road into Boulton Road on 3 January 1989, when working on the No.11A route. (D.R. Harvey)

Above: The Outer Circle bus route climbs out of the valley of Hockley Brook towards Lodge Road and HMP Winson Green. A large Edwardian church was built on a bluff at the corner of Beeton Road where the gradient slackens. Bishop Latimer's Memorial Church was consecrated in 1904, having been designed by the architect W.H. Bidlake in a Victorian Perpendicular Gothic style. Built in red brick, this large church does have a handsome square south-east tower, although the rest of the nave and chancel are rather plain. The church stood just to the north of the slightly earlier Handsworth New Road County Modern Boys and Girls School, which had been opened in 1894. (A. Spettigue)

Opposite below: After descending Boulton Road, the valley bottom of Hockley Brook is crossed and the road becomes Handsworth New Road. The road is immediately crossed by two large brick railway bridges – the one nearest to the bottom of the valley was the former Great Western Railway's mainline from Birmingham to Wolverhampton. The nearest bridge is the old L & NWR Soho, Handsworth and Perry Barr line, which, by way of the Soho Junction, served as the Birmingham avoiding line from their Stour Valley main line. Both were still in use in 2002, though the long-closed old GWR line has been used by the Midland Metro since Sunday 30 May 1999. One of the Ansaldo Transporti T69 fifty-six seat trams crosses the bridge, having just left Winson Green Station, which – in recognition of the No.11 route – was later renamed Winson Green Outer Circle. There cannot be too many tram or railway stations which are named after a bus route. (A. Spettigue)

Above: Looking down Winson Green Road towards HMP Winson Green in 2002. The Outer Circle route has been diverted over the years so that now it no longer goes down the full extent of Winson Green Road; instead, it uses Aberdeen Street, allowing passengers to alight at Dudley Road Hospital. Beyond the prison is the old centre of Winson Green, with Dolman's garage at the Foundry Road/Lodge Road junctions. Next door to Dolman's are to be found two of the oldest houses in the district, which were originally in the grounds of the nineteenth-century Winson Green House. (A. Spettigue)

Opposite above: A vanished species – shops on Winson Green Road. This photograph shows numbers 86, 88 and part of number 90, in around 1930. Herbert Cox, the baker's at number 86, also operated out of premises in nearby Dudley Road, Cape Hill and Icknield Port Road. Next door was a furniture shop and then came the butcher's, Harry Hinds. This block of twenty-seven shops between Magdala Street and Bryant Street included separate repair shops for watches, boots, cycles and mangles, as well as a wireless dealer and a Co-op. The shops were swept away at the beginning of the 1970s, destroying much of the community spirit of the district. In their place, the site has just been grassed over. (Birmingham Co-operative Society)

Above: This is the rear of a block of terraced houses in Winson Green Road, shortly before their demolition in 1972. These typical terraces are a world away from the leafy residences on the south part of the No.11 route. Winson Green is where the Outer Circle route gets closest to both the city centre and the Inner Circle route. It is only half a mile away from the Inner Circle, which crossses Dudley Road at nearby Icknield Street. (Birmingham Central Library)

The Outer Circle bus route crosses the long Winson Green Bridge, which straddles the Thomas Telford-designed Birmingham Level of the Birmingham Canal and the former L & NWR Stour Valley main railway line to Wolverhampton and the North-West. The entrance to Winson Green Station was on the eastern side of the bridge and on the inner ring of the No.11 route, which the bus is now passing. The station was closed on 15 September 1957, due in part to it not being able to compete with bus services. 2114 (JOJ 114) – a 1951 new-look front Daimler CVD6 with an M.C.C.W. body – has left behind HMP Winson Green as it travels towards the junction with Dudley Road on 24 October 1964. A curious survivor of the war can still be seen in the masked-out street lamp. (W. Ryan)

The former L & NWR Stour Valley main railway line was opened on 1 July 1852, but it was not until 1 November 1889 that Winson Green Station was opened as the second station out from New Street. Passing through the station on a Birmingham New Street to Wolverhampton High Level local service is a pair of the pioneering Derby Lightweight two-car Diesel Multiple Units, which were built in 1954 and introduced into the West Midlands in March 1956. It was quite common in the West Midlands for the coupling of two and three pairs of twin-car D.M.U.s for the heavy, local commuter traffic. However, these DMUs only used Winson Green Station for around two years before it was closed. On the bridge over the station is one of Perry Barr garage's new-look front Daimler CVD6s, fitted with Metro-Cammell bodies. This garage had buses 2108-2130 allocated to it, and they were frequent performers on the No.11 route. This bus is travelling towards HMP Winson Green, from where Charlie Wilson (one of the infamous Great Train Robbers) escaped on 12 August 1964. (R.S. Carpenter)

Above: The driver of this elderly bus pulls hard on the steering wheel as he hauls the bus out of Winson Green Road and into Dudley Road in around 1948. Although the bus has a 'lazy' destination blind, it does have a radiator slip board which displays that it has reached its destination, no doubt to the delight of its aching driver. The bus is 378 (OG 378) – a 1930 petrol-engined AEC Regent – which had been rebodied in August 1943 with an austere Brush fifty-one seater body. By this time, these buses were the only ones in the fleet with petrol engines and were allocated to Birchfield Road garage – the only one left with petrol pumps. It is a matter of some conjecture why these buses were not fitted with AEC diesel engines, as they only lasted in service until 1950. Following the bus is a little pre-war Bedford flat-bed lorry, while an Austin Cambridge 10/4 saloon of 1938 vintage is parked outside Cox's bakery shop in Dudley Road. (R.F. Mack)

Opposite above: The thirty-four-acre Summerfield Park was given to Birmingham by Lucas Chance, the nearby Smethwick-based glass manufacturer, whose house (Summerfield House) had been at the centre of the gardens. The trees on the right mark the northern side of the park, which was one of nine laid-out parks that had direct access from the Outer Circle route. The bus shelters on the right were also immediately outside Dudley Road Police Station. On 2 October 1974, in West Midland PTE days, an ex-Birmingham Daimler CVG6 with a Crossley body – 3125 (MOF 125) – travels along Dudley Road towards the left turn into City Road. In the distance is an AEC Marshall 6x4 rigid six lorry with a Leyland-designed Ergomatic cab. (J. Carroll)

Above: The corner of City Road and Dudley Road with the Lloyds Bank building. The bank was built in 1903 and it was often claimed that it was the nearest bank to Winson Green, the area being so poor that no bank thought it worthwhile to set up premises there. Even this bank probably drew most of its customers from Rotton Park and Edgbaston rather than Winson Green. Today it houses the Summerfield Community Centre, which offers advice and guidance. The elegant Edwardian fittings are still in place inside. (Andrew Maxam)

Above: A Vulcan-bodied AEC Regent 661 of the 409-443 class, which entered service in the autumn of 1930, is working on the No.11 route during the summer of 1937 and has just turned into City Road. Behind Leslie Gabb's chemist and druggist shop are the trees which mark the boundary of Summerfield Park: a lung of greenery in Dudley Road, surrounded by Victorian properties of various types, ages and architectural styles. Standing in the middle of Dudley Road being 'undertaken' by a small Morris-Commercial flat-bed van is open-balcony car 119, which was one of the West Smethwick depot's four-wheel ex-Radial truck trams. (Commercial Postcard)

Above: St Germaine's Church. This imposing brick-built church was designed by E.F. Reynolds in the Romanesque-style and, unusually, was constructed during the First World War. It was one of only two churches in the country to be consecrated during that war. Prior to this, the site was occupied by an iron-clad mission church. (Birmingham Central Library)

Opposite below: Having just been overtaken by an Austin A30 car, 3001 (LOG 301) – the lightweight Guy Arab IV with a Saunders-Roe body – crosses the traffic lights at Portland Road. This was used by the cross-city No.7 bus service, a route previously seen in this volume operating in Witton. The bus entered service on 13 November 1952, having been exhibited at the previous month's Earls Court Commercial Motor Show. The next batch of Guy Arab IVs, numbered 3003-3102, were initially going to have similar Saunders-Roe bodies, but the devil was in the detail and the contract was never signed, leaving these 100 buses caught up in a protracted delivery from Metro-Cammell which took sixteen months to complete. The unique 3001 leaves the suburb of Rotton Park and enters Edgbaston. This is City Road, reputedly the straightest and longest road in Birmingham, which had been laid out in the last decade of Queen Victoria's reign. (A.D. Broughall)

Above: The Edgbaston end of City Road was lined with a mixture of pre-First World War detached and semi-detached houses, which were generally of better quality than those at the Dudley Road end, illustrating how the social structure of those days was reflected in the location and suburban address of the day. Long-time performers on the Outer Circle were the splendid Brush-bodied Leyland Titan D2/1s of 1948, which were usually between seventeen and nineteen years old by the time they were withdrawn. 1739 (HOV 739) passes the junction with Wadhurst Road as it approaches the extensive site occupied by the George Dixon Schools on the opposite side of the road in around 1954. The bus is still equipped with trafficators (which would be replaced by flashing indicators from around 1958) and it is carrying advertisements for the long-forgotten Ecko radios, which were considered to be amongst the best available at the time. (P. Tizard)

Opposite below: A comparative rarity on the Outer Circle route until the demise of Corporation-run buses was to see one of the ten prototype Daimler Fleetline CRG6LXs (which by this time were allocated to Perry Barr garage) operating. These Metro-Cammell-bodied buses always retained their triple destination boxes, which in turn meant that they could not be operated without a conductor. Recently repainted in West Midlands PTE livery, the first of the ten – 3241 (241 DOC) – has travelled the full length of City Road and stands at the tree-lined junction with Sandon Road. (L. Mason)

Left: Schoolchildren have become major users of the Outer Circle route in recent years as they travel across the city to their favoured schools, and the bus stop outside George Dixon Schools is a major morning and afternoon destination. The schools were opened as far back as 1906 as City of Birmingham Council schools. The secondary school was later a grammar school and is now the George Dixon International School and Sixth Form Centre. Both the primary and the international schools take pupils from a wide mix of backgrounds and ethnicities. Two famous figures in the arts world – Kenneth Tynan, the film and theatre critic, and Michael Balcon, the film producer – attended the schools. Balcon's autobiography *Michael Balcon Presents* contains an interesting few pages on school life before the First World War. (Birmingham Central Library)

During a late snow flurry in April 1977, 3129 (MOF 129) – a Daimler CVG6 with a Crossley H30/25R body, which by now was almost twenty-four years old – comes down the gently curving slope of Barnsley Road, having passed the large late-Victorian semi-detached houses lining both sides of the road. It is working on the No.11A route and is already braking for the Hagley Road junction, where (unbeknown to most of the bus passengers) they are crossing the flood plain of the Chad Brook Valley, which also marked the Birmingham-Bearwood boundary. In the background is the tall nave of Barnsley Road's Methodist Church. (D.R. Harvey)

The lost art of jumping off a bus which is stuck in a queue of traffic is amply displayed here in Hagley Road, as 459 (OV 4459) – a petrol-engined AEC Regent 661 – approaches the end of its journey. The bus is showing the destination display 'Hagley Road', although it will turn into Lordswood Road to terminate at the Bundy Clock alongside the Kings Head. This former Short Brothers piano-front-bodied bus had been rebodied by Brush in 1943, and by 1948 (despite the body being only five years old when it was photographed) was restricted to peak hour extra services because of its heavy steering and extremely low fuel consumption (S.E. Letts)

The Outer Circle route was diverted away from Barnsley Road to serve the Bearwood shopping centre after the deregulation of the bus services in October 1986. As a result, Bearwood Road became the only part of the Outer Circle route to be outside the City boundary. The bus is 2980 (E980 VUK) – a 1988 MCW Metrobus Mk II, with a Metro-Cammell H43/30F body – which is travelling away from the centre of Bearwood on the No.11A route on 3 January 1989. It is passing the long row of shops which are continuous from Adkins Lane, via Bearwood bus station, to Anderson Road. These premises were built as houses in the 1890s, but within fifteen years they had lost their small walled gardens and become shops. (D.R. Harvey)

There are plenty of parks to travel to on the Outer Circle, and Lightswood Park is the last one we meet on our journey round. Along with Handsworth, Swanshurst and Rookery Parks, Lightswood Park would have been a favourite destination on summer days in the past, although the impression today is that not many people actually take the No.11 to the city's parks. These youngsters are enjoying Lightswood Park in August 1954, which celebrates its centenary in June 2004. (Birmingham Central Library)

The shopping centre in Bearwood Road contained some of the best-known pre-war retail outlets in the West Midlands. The end shops that are visible include George Mason's grocery and provision merchants (outside which was the Bearwood terminus of the No.29 route), Dewhurst's butcher's shop, England's shoe shop (with its canvas blind extended) and Smarts the pork butcher's. Out of sight, further up the row, was the Birmingham Co-op, Freeman, Hardy & Willis (another boot and shoe retailer), Wrenson's grocery store and a large Woolworths. The tram tracks in Bearwood Road and those in the right foreground, for the No.34 Hagley Road tram route, were never joined up despite over a dozen attempts to extend the Birmingham & Midland Tramway Company's Bearwood route to Quinton and Halesowen. The Bearwood Road tram service had been opened on 24 November 1904, while the never popular No.34 service was opened by Birmingham Corporation Tramways on 5 February 1913, after much opposition from the influential Calthorpe Estate and its well-heeled residents, and closed on Tuesday 9 September 1930. Behind the white-coated traffic policeman is the corner of Lightswood Park, while in Beech Lane, in the shadow of the trees, is a group of people waiting to catch a Midland Red bus to Halesowen or Stourbridge. The Outer Circle bus service turned left from Hagley Road into Lordswood Road. (Birmingham Central Library)

The Kings Head was the first public house in Birmingham beyond the Ivy Bush along Hagley Road. This was because the Gough-Calthorpe family, rather like the Cadburys at Bournville, would not allow public houses on their well-managed Calthorpe Estate. As far as their restrictions went, they could not prevent the rebuilding of an existing inn when the Holte Brewery signed such an agreement. The pub, attractively designed by Holte's own architects, Owen and Ward, in a mixture of mock-Tudor half-timbering, brick and terracotta, was re-opened in 1905. (Birmingham Central Library)

204 (OP 233), one of the first generation of double-deckers to operate on the No.11 bus service, stands alongside the Kings Head public house in Lordswood Road. By now fitted with pneumatic tyres, this AEC 504 with a top-covered, outside staircase and Buckingham H26/26RO body entered service on 7 September 1926. The driver, wearing a trenchcoat, stands at the rear of the bus, talking to his conductor alongside the Bundy Clock, having endured a drive around the route in the open cab of his charge. (N.N. Forbes/N.T.M. Crich)

Early on a sunny afternoon in the summer of 1952, 2489 (JOJ 489) stands in Lordswood Road alongside the Kings Head public house, while the crew wait for their leaving time and clock-in at the Bundy Clock. The bus is a Crossley DD42/7 (chassis number 95177), which was fitted with an 8.598 litre Crossley HOE7/5B down-draught engine and a Crossley H30/24R body, which weighed an extremely heavy 8 tons 6 cwt 2 qts. 2489 was one of the 100 pioneering buses which were the first in the country to enter service with the new-look concealed radiator. The bus entered service on 1 July 1950 and would remain in service until 31 March 1969. All this detail is highly relevant as this bus has been preserved in this condition by one of the authors of this book, and this is one of the earliest photographs of his Crossley in service. (D.R. Harvey)

An inspector casts a malevolent eye from behind the bus shelter as 3832 (NOV 832G) stands at the bus shelter in Lordswood Road, with the Kings Head public house in the background. These buses were the very last complete batch of vehicles delivered to Birmingham City Transport. They were Daimler Fleetline CRG6LXs and were the first in the fleet to have a two-door layout and a central forward ascending staircase, neither feature being popular with either passengers or crews. The order for the bodies for these buses was meant to go to Metro-Cammell, but because of industrial difficulties, the contract went to Park Royal. 3832 (NOV 832G) entered service on 14 January 1969. When new, these buses were equipped for two-man operation – they were not fitted for driver-only operation until after the formation of the PTE. (J.C. Walker)

By way of contrast, a member of the first post-war delivery of buses – 1537 (GOE 537), a 1948 Daimler CVA6 with a fifty-four seat Metro-Cammell body – is unloading at the bus stop in Lordswood Road before moving off to turn right into Hagley Road. This bus was one of Harborne garage's vehicles and as late as 1961, when the bus would only have around another two years' service left to do, would be in all-day service, despite having to undertake the rigours of the No.11 route with only a small 7.58 litre AEC engine under the bonnet. Following the bus towards the Kings Head traffic island is a BMW Isetta three-wheeler bubble car; these were all the rage until largely killed off by the Austin Mini. (R. Weaver)

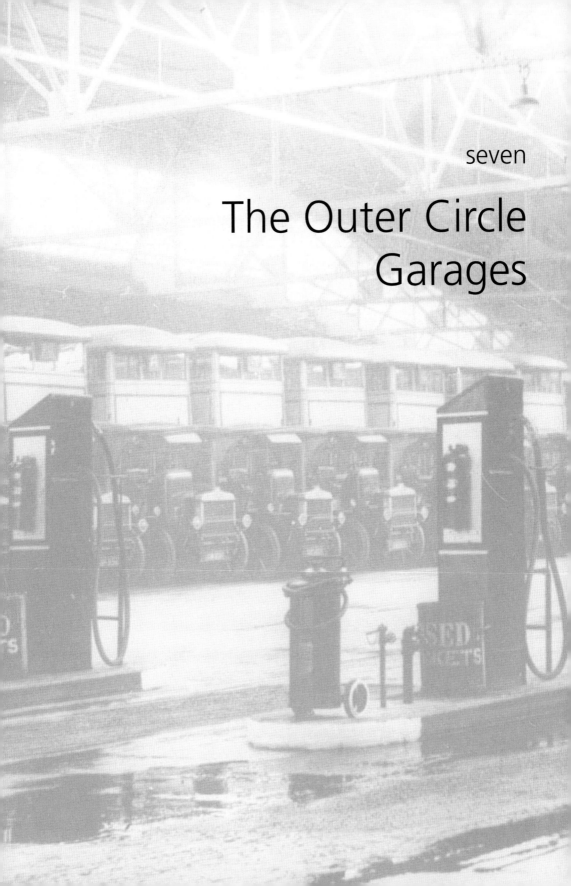

seven

The Outer Circle Garages

The first purpose-built bus garage for the Transport Department was at Lonsdale Road, Harborne. It was opened on 12 October 1926 and had the capacity to hold 100 buses. In May 1929, the line-up of AEC 504s reveal that the fleet has yet to be converted to pneumatic tyres. Most of the buses – including 137 (OM 9551) of 1925 vintage and 187 (OP 216), built the following year – have Short H26/26RO bodies. The bus with the slightly more domed roof is 197 (OP 226), which has a similar capacity body built by Thompson, a Lincolnshire-based bodybuilder. By the end of the year, the first of the piano-front AEC Regents would arrive and literally revolutionise the Corporation's bus fleet. Alas, the Outer Circle would not get these new buses for a couple of years, despite passenger complaints in the local press. (D.R. Harvey Collection)

Typical of the buses used on the No.11 route in the twenty-five years after the Second World War is this selection parked in Lonsdale Road. Although, strictly speaking, this was the back of Harborne garage, as the offices and stores were at the Serpentine Road end, the Lonsdale Road end was much more accessible from the centre of Harborne and was therefore used for buses leaving the garage at the start of the day and as the entrance for returning buses, as the fuel pumps were also at this end of the garage. Parked facing Lordswood Road is one of Washwood Heath garage's Daimler CVD6s – 2724 (JOJ 724) –which had done a half-turn on the No.11 route. Washwood Heath, along with Hockley, Cotteridge, Quinton and Lea Hall garages, put buses out onto the Circle, especially during the peak times. 1726 (HOV 726) – a Leyland Titan PD2/1, with a Brush H30/24R body – is another interloper, this time from Perry Barr, while peaking out of the gloom of Harborne garage is 2513 (JOJ 513), an indigenous new-look front Crossley DD42/7, with a Crossley body, which entered service on 1 September 1950. (A.D. Broughall)

Above: The premises in Harborne Lane were formally opened on 8 July 1927 as both a tram depot and a bus garage. It became operational four days later when the old Bournbrook depot was closed. Selly Oak operated on the No.11 route for its first operational year until Acocks Green garage was opened, and again from 1935 until 1949. Selly Oak was designed by the Buildings Superintendent of the Tramways Department, F.J. Hopkins, and cost £37,000. It had the capacity for eighty tramcars, while about thirty-five buses could be housed. In 1947, the first thirty of the GOE-registered Daimler CVG6s were allocated to Selly Oak's bus garage to replace the 1934 Daimler COG5s, which had been there since new. 1562 (GOE 562), one of these CVG6s, stands on Selly Oak forecourt on a rainy day in company with two others of the batch, as well as one of the AOG-registered 1934 COG5s. On the tram side of the forecourt is Brush totally-enclosed car 588, with Brush Burnley bogies at the entrance to the depot, while about to leave the depot is car 521, a 1913-built U.E.C. bogie car with an eight-windowed top cover fitted in 1929. On the extreme left is car 842, the revolutionary lightweight Short-bodied tramcar, which entered service in November 1929 and ran all its life from Cotteridge depot. (D.R. Harvey Collection)

Opposite above: In June 1928, Acocks Green garage was opened. It was situated on Fox Hollies Road opposite Westley Road, with an initial capacity for fifty buses. Originally, it had AEC 504s and 507s, but it quickly received some of the first Brush-bodied AEC Regent 661s to be delivered to the Corporation. By 1939, Acocks Green had received a variety of Daimler COG5s, which were only replaced by the influx of exposed-radiator Daimler CVD6s and later by fifty exposed-radiator Crossley DD42/7s. In the winter of 1950, 1230 (FOF 230) – a 1939 Daimler COG5 with a Metro-Cammell H30/24R body – is fitted with a radiator muff. It stands inside the garage along with several other pre-war Daimlers and, on the left, one of the then brand-new Crossleys. (D.R. Harvey Collection)

Above: The official opening of Perry Barr garage took place on Tuesday 16 February 1932, and within eighteen months the fleet had been augmented by the last seventeen of the Morris-Commercial Imperial double-deckers. These had a style of Metro-Cammell body only perpetuated in Birmingham on the fifty Leyland TTBD2 trolleybuses which opened the Coventry Road service and the solitary pre-war Guy Arab. In October 1933, six of these new Morrises were lined up in Wellhead Lane yard, including, from left to right: 551, 549, 539, 540, 547 and 543, with matching OC-registrations. (Morris-Commercial)

When Perry Barr garage was partially opened in August 1931, the garage had the second largest unsupported roof in the world, which allowed buses complete access to all parts of the garage. It eventually had the capacity to hold 160 buses, and was always involved in operating a major share of the buses on the No.11 route. The garage was known in the department as Wellhead Lane, in order to differentiate it from the Birchfield Road garage in the centre of Perry Barr. Parked inside the garage in around 1964 are two of the long-lived Brush-bodied Leyland Titan PD2/1s – 1715 (HOV 715) and 1733 (HOV 733) – and two Crossley DD42/7s with Crossley bodies, one of which is 2377 (JOJ 377). It is interesting that both the Crossleys, which were also operated by Acocks Green and Harborne garage on the Outer Circle route, and the Leylands had synchromesh gearboxes, which were less common than the Wilson fluid-flywheel pre-selector gearboxes fitted to the Daimlers and all but six of the post-war Guy Arabs. (A. Yates)

Standing at the entrance to Birchfield Road garage on 5 October 1950 is 399 (OG 399). This is one of the fifty piano-front AEC Regent 661s, built with a variety of different makes of body between 1929 and 1931, which were fitted with Ministry of War Transport utility-style bodies built by Brush, unusually featuring a straight staircase. The bus is parked alongside the petrol pumps, which were the last ones to be found in any of the Corporation's bus garages. The garage was originally built as a tramcar depot by Handsworth UDC and subsequently led a chequered career as a bus garage, frequently being used as an overflow for the nearby Wellhead Lane. Petrol bus operation ended on New Year's Eve 1950, and for many years the garage became the home of the early Daimler CVA6s, which seemed permanently to work on the peak-hour No.25 route to Kingstanding. Birchfield Road closed as an operational garage in August 1966 and later became an ambulance depot. (R. Wilson)

Acknowledgements

The authors are grateful to the many photographers – both those acknowledged in the text and many other unknown photographers – who have contributed to this volume. Special thanks are due to Roger Carpenter for access to his extensive files of railway photographs, and to Tony Hall and Barry Ware for their anecdotes and valuable factual contributions about the Outer Circle bus route. In addition, Peter Townsend of Silver Link Publishing was most helpful in retrieving a lost photograph electronically at very short notice. Finally, thanks are also due to Diana Harvey for proof-reading sections of the manuscript and supplying coffee to these three writers.

Picture Credits

The photographs in this book have come from two main sources. Nearly every historical picture of a bus working on the No.11 route has come from the collection of David Harvey and many of these are being published for the first time. The modern-day pictures were kindly supplied by Anthony Spettigue, while many of the pictures of important buildings and street scenes came from the various collections belonging to the Local Studies section of Birmingham Central Reference Library, where they can easily be accessed. The library is always happy to receive copies of images of Birmingham to add to the extensive collections held there.